# THE GROWTH OF THE WORLD CHURCH

# THE GROWTH OF THE WORLD CHURCH

*The Story of the*
*Modern Missionary Movement*

by

ERNEST A. PAYNE
M.A., D.D.

EDINBURGH HOUSE PRESS
2 EATON GATE, LONDON, S.W.1

★   ★   ★

MACMILLAN AND CO. LIMITED
ST. MARTIN'S STREET, LONDON
1955

MACMILLAN AND COMPANY LIMITED
*London Bombay Calcutta Madras Melbourne*

THE MACMILLAN COMPANY OF CANADA LIMITED
*Toronto*

ST MARTIN'S PRESS INC
*New York*

*Printed in Great Britain by*
THE GARDEN CITY PRESS LIMITED LETCHWORTH HERTFORDSHIRE

To G.W.H.

# CONTENTS

# CONTENTS

# FOREWORD

AN ATTEMPT is made in the pages that follow to give some account of the way in which the Christian religion has spread during the last two hundred and fifty years, and particularly since the birth of the modern missionary movement. Attention is mainly concentrated on the work of the British missionary societies and some of their leading figures. The aim has been to set the founders and pioneers against the background of their time; to show how those of many different Christian traditions shared in the revival of missionary zeal; and to trace the gradual shift of emphasis of recent years from the individual and the society to the Church itself, whether in this land or overseas. The work of the great American and Continental societies and that of the Roman Catholic Church are alluded to only incidentally.

The standard histories of the British societies, such as those by Pascoe, Lovett, Stock, Canton, and Findlay, have been, of course, invaluable, and my debt to them is obvious; but I have also used material not to be found in the official histories. By permission of the Edinburgh House Press I have made use of substantial portions of a book I wrote some ten years ago which was published by the United Council for Missionary Education under the title *The Church Awakes*. Three of the chapters are, however, completely new and the others have been drastically revised.

An increasing number of school syllabuses include sections on the growth of the Church in modern times. It is my hope that what I have written may be useful to teachers and senior scholars, as well as of interest to the general reader. I hope also that it may prove a stimulus and challenge to further reading and study and to a sharing in the unfinished evangelistic task of the Church.

ERNEST A. PAYNE.

# CHAPTER I

# END OR BEGINNING?

" To be together in action, and to be together in
desire, for Christ's sake, may at least be a beginning
of the fulfilment of His prayer that all may be one."
G. K. A. Bell, *Christian Unity*. Hodder & Stoughton,
1948, p. 190.

I

AT THE CORONATION of Her Majesty Queen Elizabeth
in June 1953, one of the royal visitors who attracted
special attention was Queen Salote of Tonga. Both
in Westminster Abbey, where she made a truly
regal entry, and in the procession afterwards through
the streets of London, where in spite of the rain she
quickly made friendly contact with the crowd, she
showed herself an unusual personality. At the time, not
many who saw Queen Salote thought of her as a living
symbol of the now world-wide character of the
Christian Church. In the weeks that followed, however, as she journeyed to different parts of Britain, many
came to know that she was a third-generation Christian
and discovered how vital and eager was her interest in
other members of the Christian Church. Here from
one of the remote islands of the South Seas was a ruler
whose adherence to the Christian religion shone forth
as clearly and strongly as that of Queen Elizabeth
herself. That she proved to be a Methodist gave an
added piquancy to the sudden realization that came to

many of the extent and character of the Church of the twentieth century.

A few weeks after Queen Elizabeth's coronation, at a critical moment in the negotiations for an armistice in Korea, a leading member of the staff of the World Council of Churches set off by air from New York for Seoul. He wished to talk to Mr Syngman Rhee as one Christian to another, for the President of the South Korean Republic, enigmatic and controversial figure as he has been from the standpoint of international politics, is known in his own country as a staunch Christian, a member of one of the Presbyterian Churches.

These are but two illustrations from the many which might be offered of that " great new fact of our time " to which Dr William Temple alluded in his enthronement sermon in Canterbury Cathedral in 1942. " God," he said, " has been building up a Christian fellowship which now extends into almost every nation, binds citizens of them all together in true unity and mutual love. No human agency has planned this. It is the result of the great missionary enterprise of the last hundred and fifty years." In the fourth century of our era, Cyril of Jerusalem offered a fourfold definition of what is meant by the word " catholicity " as applied to the Church: its extension throughout the world, the wholeness of its gospel, its unifying power over " all sorts and conditions of men," and its capacity to heal every sin of soul and body. The most dramatic and convincing proof of the first and third of those claims has come in our own day. The Christian faith now has adherents in almost every race and nation. No religion has ever before spread so widely through the earth. In the fellowship of the Church

Universal, moreover, there are ties that are proving themselves stronger than the divisive forces of class, of nationality, of race, of ideology and even of long-established ecclesiastical custom and tradition.

In the last years of his life, Archbishop Temple played an important part in the planning of the World Council of Churches. Its creation became one of the enterprises dearest to his heart. At the time of his enthronement seventy-six churches had signified their intention of joining. When, in 1948, four years after Dr Temple's lamented death, the World Council actually came into existence and held a first assembly in Amsterdam, representatives from no less than one hundred and forty-four Churches came together. Some of them were Churches with a long history—the ancient Church of Abyssinia, for example, the Coptic Church of Egypt, the Orthodox Syrian Church of India, the Orthodox Church of Greece. The Church of England was represented, and the various Churches of the Anglican communion overseas. There were delegates from the Lutheran and Reformed Churches of Europe and America and from the great Free Churches—Baptist, Congregationalist and Methodist. There were Waldensians, Moravians and Mennonites. But from many points of view the most striking group of representatives were those who came from the Church of Christ in China, the Church of South India, the Church of Christ in Japan, the Church of Christ in Siam, the United Evangelical Church of the Philippines —that is, the delegates of the so-called " younger Churches," which have come into existence in the last one hundred and fifty years.

Since the Amsterdam Assembly, the now world-wide character of the Church has become even clearer. The new Christian leadership that is emerging is international in character. Sixty years ago "native Christians" were occasionally brought to Britain and were treated almost as trophies or exhibits. In 1933, however, the Churches of India, Burma and Ceylon sent a mission of fellowship to this country and a similar group of leaders from the younger Churches visited Britain early in 1939. Such visits by individuals and teams have now become almost as familiar as the presence here of Asian and African political leaders. In the varied activities of the World Council of Churches, men and women of the most varied nationality, race and denominational affiliation serve as colleagues. Its committees meet, now in Geneva, now in Toronto, now in Lucknow and now in some other part of the world.

The World Council of Churches is a striking demonstration of "the great new fact of our time." It is not, however, a complete expression of it. The Roman Church, with its millions of adherents of many races and lands, stands aloof from the Council; its exclusive claim to truth and authority still makes association and co-operation with other Christians almost impossible, but it should be noted that when new cardinals were created in 1946 they included representatives of all five continents, among them a Chinese. A number of the Orthodox Churches remain outside the World Council, most of them from political rather than religious motives. Certain groups of Protestants are suspicious of the Council on theological grounds, some wish for a more lengthy, definite and Calvinistic doctrinal basis, while others make on their own account exclusive claims. These three groups—Roman, Orthodox and Protestant—comprise a very large number of the

Christians of the world. They must be kept in mind in assessing the total strength of the Church. Reliable statistics are difficult to obtain. Professing Christians are probably more numerous than ever before. They are certainly more widely spread.

## II

" It is as yet too early to say whether the Christian penetration of the non-European world is profound or superficial."[1] The words were written in 1946 in a review of the last of the seven volumes of Professor K. S. Latourette's great *History of the Expansion of Christianity*. That history surveyed the spread of the faith from the first to the twentieth century and was based upon many years of extensive and intensive research. The author's final conclusion was an optimistic one. He believed that " in geographic extent, in movements issuing from it, and in its effect upon the race, in the nineteenth century Christianity had a far larger place in human history than at any previous time,"[2] and that a forward march continued on into the twentieth century so that it could be said that " when one views the entire globe geographically, Christianity is stronger in 1941, and in a better position to influence the human race than it was in 1914."[3]

Such a judgment depends, in large part, on the place of vantage from which the observer is looking out over the human scene and on the conclusion he has come to regarding the general movement of affairs. Such an observer is inevitably influenced by his geographical and cultural background and by his ideology and faith. Dr Latourette carried out his studies from Yale

---

[1] *Times Literary Supplement,* August 3rd, 1946.
[2] Op. cit., v. p. 1.    [3] *The Unquenchable Light,* p. 113.

University as Professor of Missions and Oriental History. The assessment of the situation from London, Berlin or Moscow, or from Delhi or Peking, even if made by a Christian of equal knowledge, might be slightly different. More important, however, is the pattern or lack of pattern which a student comes to believe he discerns in the wider processes of history.

Dr Latourette, as a result of his studies, offers this judgment on the progress of the faith:

" The course of Christianity in the history of mankind has been somewhat like that of an incoming tide. As one stands on the shore and watches the tide sweep in, he sees that each major wave carries the waters a little higher than did its predecessor. Each retreat from a major wave carries the flood a little less farther back than did the one before it. So with Christianity. . . . At the outset was the advance of the first five centuries. Then came the longest and most disheartening of all the recessions, roughly from A.D. 500 to A.D. 950. This was succeeded by a forward push which stretched from A.D. 950 to A.D. 1350. After this ensued another retreat, briefer and not so extensive as its predecessor, from A.D. 1350 to A.D. 1500. The next surge of the tide, from A.D. 1500 to A.D. 1750, made Christianity more of a factor in human affairs than did either of the ones before it. There then came, from A.D. 1750 to A.D. 1815, what was not so much a recession as a pause in the onward sweep of Christianity, and in the two generations embraced by the period, to those who had eyes to see, Christianity was gathering momentum for another advance. That advance, from A.D. 1815 to A.D. 1914, we have termed the great century, for it was the era in which Christianity for the first time became world-wide. In the three decades which were inaugurated by A.D. 1914 progress became less rapid and severe losses were encountered. Yet the years were ones of significant gains."[1]

These sentences present a striking and hopeful picture of Christian history. How far is it correct?

Our chief concern here is with the developments in the past few centuries. Many would set them forth in much gloomier shades than does Dr Latourette. Since the Reformation, they would say, Christianity has been weakened by internal divisions. The apparent expansion of the Church in the nineteenth century was part of British and American imperialism and the spread of Western culture. Even while it was going on, the Christian faith was losing its hold on the peoples of Europe, and the losses here outweighed the gains elsewhere. The nineteenth century was " the heyday of internationalism, cosmopolitanism and world missions,"[2] but that period is now over, and its legatees have been secular humanism and atheistic Communism.

At a conference in Malvern in 1941, Mr J. Middleton Murry asserted that " the Christian Church is weaker today than it has ever been since it was founded." What has happened since? The men of the Kremlin have tightened their hold on satellite countries and have persecuted and imprisoned the leaders of the Churches, making innocuous the witness of those who remain. China has become Communist and the Christian Churches there, never very strong in relation to the number of the population, have had to see and even encourage the departure of all foreign missionaries

---

[1] *History of the Expansion of Christianity*, vii, pp. 418-19.
[2] Quoted by A. G. Hebert, *The Throne of David*, p. 94 n.

and to sever their connection with the Churches of America and the West. Though the new India is committed to religious freedom, it is also growingly hostile to the activities of missionaries from overseas. In many lands a rising tide of nationalism goes hand in hand with a resurgence of Hinduism, Buddhism and Islam, or, as in Africa, with that of more primitive religions. When the Anglican bishop in Iran was expelled from that land in 1953, he made a confession that applies to the situation over wide areas of Asia and Africa:

" What the Church has to do—and has largely failed to do—is to convince the world that Christianity is a universal religion with a message for all mankind at every level. It has to clear people's minds of the idea that it is inherently connected with secular western civilization, which is now under suspicion in the Middle East."[1]

So one might go on, building up a case which suggests not the continued expansion of the Christian faith, but its gradual suppression and disappearance in many of the lands where it had gained a foothold.

The expansion of the Church in the nineteenth century and the early decades of the twentieth century was, as Dr Temple said, the result of the great missionary activity of the Churches of Western Europe and America. " In the closing years of the eighteenth century," says Dr Latourette, " and swelling to full flood in the nineteenth and the opening years of the twentieth century, came a new access of life which was to make of these decades the most remarkable era in the history of the expansion of Christianity."[2] What-

[1] *Church Times*, July 31st, 1953. It is reassuring to know that in 1954 the Bishop was allowed to return.    [2] *History*, i, pp. xix-xx.

ever the causes and whatever the future may hold in store this cannot be denied, nor the personal daring which accompanied the new upsurging of life.

Missionaries do not often capture the public imagination. They have often been the butt of ridicule. Occasionally a Livingstone or a Knibb, a Wilfred Grenfell, a Schweitzer, a C. F. Andrews or a Michael Scott may become a familiar figure, sometimes notorious and the centre of controversy. But for the most part missionaries do not figure in the news. When a little group of " civilian " prisoners arrived from Korea by way of Peking and Moscow in the early summer of 1953, it was a surprise to many to hear that they included an Irish Roman Catholic priest, an Anglican bishop and a Salvation Army officer. Yet the group was in many ways typical of those who might have been found up till recent times in almost any part of Asia, Africa or the South Seas. It is the work of men like these that has brought into existence the Younger Churches. There are said to have been in 1925 some 28,000 Protestant missionaries working in different parts of the world, and some 22,000 Roman Catholics. Whether or not the number has markedly declined since then—there has certainly been a redistribution— there is still a very considerable company of men and women at work as Christian preachers, educators, doctors and nurses in lands other than their own.

From some lands they are now shut out, in others their foothold is precarious. Everywhere their status in the Younger Churches is changing. " ' Foreign Missions ' have had their day," says Mr Cecil Northcott,[1] and this not only because of resurgent nationalism, the revival of indigenous cultures and the violent change

[1] *British Weekly*, July 9th, 1953.

in the balance of relations between East and West, but also because of the growth of the Church and because large numbers of missionaries are aware that in some places they may now be a liability to the Young Christian communities. The Churches of Asia and Africa are growing to maturity, as is shown by the part they play in the World Council of Churches. In nearly every land some section of the Church is beyond the " missions " stage. Even where there is still great weakness and immaturity, missionaries and the societies that send and support them have the difficult task of determining the time when and the manner in which it is best to devolve responsibility and, perhaps, withdraw personnel as well as money.

What is comprehensively described as the Ecumenical Movement is also transforming ideas about foreign missions. The World Council of Churches is a product of this movement, but the movement is something wider and deeper than any institution or organization. For nearly half a century Churches of many different traditions have been busily engaged in forming links with one another on many different planes and in many different spheres. They are engaged not only in a sustained conversation with one another, but in practical co-operation at many points. One of the results has been a new emphasis on the Church, its worship, its unity and its mission. The great missionary enterprise of the nineteenth century created its own instruments and organizations. These were often separate from the rest of the life of the Church, supported by devoted groups of enthusiasts. The missionary societies themselves, quite apart from the reminders they receive from the Younger Churches, are realizing that they have to become more closely integrated with the total witness and life of the Church at home. Equally it is necessary for each church member, whether here or overseas, to be made to realize that by his membership he is committed to the worldwide missionary task of the Church. The very word " Ecumenical " may be said to cover " everything that relates to the whole task of the whole Church to bring the Gospel to the whole world."[1]

All these things suggest that we are at the end of one epoch of Christian history and at the beginning of another. Whatever the future holds, there can be no doubt that the past two hundred years have formed a notable chapter in the long story of the Church. We shall better understand the present situation if we know how it developed. We may learn something of what the Christian strategy of the future should be, if we trace the way in which the Christian faith has been carried overseas. It is with the non-Roman Churches that we shall be primarily concerned in the following pages, but it would be wrong not to recall first two or three of the remarkable figures who, influenced by those movements in the Roman Church which are usually described as the Counter-Reformation, carried the banner of the Church to other continents. There were other forerunners of the extensive missionary activity of the past one hundred and fifty years—one or two, but only one or two, of the Protestant leaders of the Reformation epoch, a few, but only a few, of the Puritans, some of the more devoted chaplains of the Society for the Propagation of the Gospel, the little group of German missionaries who went to Tranquebar,

---

[1] *The Calling of the Church to Mission and Unity: The First Six Years, 1948-1954*, p. 126. (From a statement of the Central Committee of the World Council of Churches, Rolle, Switzerland, 1951.)

and the Moravians. Some brief account of these forerunners must be given before we turn to the astonishing missionary awakening that came towards the close of the eighteenth century and resulted in the formation of a score or more of missionary societies, whose work during the past century and a half has carried the Christian religion to every part of the world.

# CHAPTER II

# FORERUNNERS OF ADVANCE

" One loving spirit sets another on fire."
Augustine, *Confessions*, IV. 44.

I

THE PROTESTANT CHURCHES from the sixteenth to the
eighteenth centuries showed a strange lack of concern
for the heathen world. Their blindness and indifference were the more remarkable in view of the widespread missionary activity of the Roman Church in the
generations immediately after the great burst of
exploration which marks the transition from the
medieval to the modern world.

Dr Latourette has suggested six reasons for the
greater extent and prominence of Roman Catholic
missions, particularly those of the sixteenth and seventeenth centuries. Protestantism, he says, was too
engrossed with its own theological and ecclesiastical
affairs to have leisure for non-Christians outside
Western Europe. Moreover, several of its leaders
expressly disavowed any obligation to carry the
Christian message to non-Christians. Thirdly, there
was inevitable preoccupation with the wars that raged
in Europe during those centuries, especially those which
involved Germany, France and the Netherlands.
Fourthly, the comparative indifference of Protestant
governments to the religious condition of their subjects
overseas was in striking contrast to the policy of the

Roman Catholic powers. Fifthly, Protestants lacked any equivalent to the orders of monks who for more than a thousand years had been the chief agents in propagating the Christian faith. Sixthly, and most important of all in the judgment of Dr Latourette, during the seventeenth and eighteenth centuries Protestants had relatively little touch with non-Christian peoples, save for the slave populations of the West Indies and the American colonies, and the Red Indians of North America.[1]

The chief navigating and exploring nations of the day were Spain and Portugal. Though Columbus was himself of Genoese birth, it was as a Spanish admiral that he discovered America. It was the Portuguese Vasco da Gama who sailed round Africa and opened up the new route to India and the Far East. It was natural that the first missionaries to the vast territories thus made accessible should be Spaniards and Portuguese, and therefore that they should be Roman Catholics. There was, moreover, what H. A. L. Fisher has described as " an atmosphere of exalted expectation "[2] at the time of Columbus' discoveries, and this was shared by the leaders of the Roman Church. It was not only the desire for wealth and power that moved men, prevalent as these motives undoubtedly were.

II

No one can be unmoved by the story of Francis Xavier, " the one missionary of the Roman Church whom all Christendom honours."[3] Born the year that Columbus died, the son of a noble house of Navarre, a

---

[1] Latourette, iii, pp. 25 f.    [2] *History of Europe*, p. 485.
[3] Stock, i. p. 17. G. J. Brodrick, *Saint Francis Xavier*. London, 1953.

graduate of Paris, gifted, eloquent, impetuous and of great personal charm, he was one of the little group of seven who, in 1534, under the leadership of Ignatius Loyola, began the Society of Jesus. He was then twenty-eight years old, and Europe was in the throes of the Reformation. Seven years later Xavier was sent by his leader as chaplain missionary to Goa, the Portuguese settlement on the west coast of India, and into the remaining ten years of his life he crowded journeyings which have given him an imperishable fame. India, Malacca, Ceylon, Cochin, Japan, India again, and then the gateway of China—everywhere he went with his bell, calling men and women together for the simplest kind of instruction, spending himself for the lowliest and most degraded, as well as for the learned and influential, for the low-caste pearl-fishers of the Malabar coast and the learned Buddhist priests of Japan. " It is not a single province of Palestine, which we were seeking, that God has given you, but the Indies —a whole world of people and nations. . . . Kindle those unknown nations with the flame that burns within you."[1] So Loyola had written to his friend at the beginning of the enterprise, and with unquenchable ardour, in face of many obstacles and disappointments, Xavier sought to carry out his commission, until, alone on a little island off Canton, dreaming of missionary pioneering in the Celestial Empire, his eager spirit was called home.

Xavier's missionary methods are easy to criticize. He left little for others to build upon. During all his missionary activities he made no attempt to learn any language understood by those to whom he preached, relying entirely upon interpreters who were often far

[1] Quoted by A. H. Small, *For the Faith*, p. 21.

from efficient. He frequently made use of the secular
powers to assist his objects. But his restless and intense
devotion to the cause of Christ caught the imagination
of the sixteenth century, and has remained an inspiration ever since. The evangelicals of the eighteenth
century viewed Roman Catholic missions with deep
suspicion, if not active hostility, but the memory of
Xavier they could not but honour. Even Melvill
Horne had to confess that Francis was " himself a
host . . . his labours were wonderful . . . he appears a
man of the first magnitude,"[1] while Henry Martyn,
who during his first days in Calcutta read the life of the
Jesuit pioneer, confessed himself " exceedingly roused
at the astonishing example of that great saint."[2]

Francis Xavier stood in a class by himself. But others
followed him. In an age of restless exploration " Rome
marched forward with the world's advancing boun-
daries." No doubt the motives of the secular and
ecclesiastical potentates who directed Roman missions
were very mixed, and there are most unsatisfactory
and unattractive episodes on record, but there was
throughout a wealth of personal devotion, sincere and
disciplined—devotion to the Church and to Jesus
Christ—which make the story of Roman Catholic
efforts in Asia and the Americas a challenge and a
rebuke. Matteo Ricci followed Xavier to China;
Robert de Nobili worked in India; Bartholomeo Las
Casas became " The Protector of the Indians " or
" The Apostle of the Indies." The story of the last
named is a revealing one. In 1498 he and his father
sailed with Columbus on the latter's third voyage to
the West Indies. Las Casas was then twenty-four.

[1] *Letters on Missions*, pp. 29-30.
[2] *Journals and Letters of the Rev. Henry Martyn*, July 22nd, 1806.

Twelve years later, out in Haiti, he was ordained as a priest, and settled in Cuba. He had at one time enslaved a number of the Indian inhabitants, but he became more and more concerned for their welfare, championing their cause in Spain as well as in the Indies. Unfortunately, one of his remedies—which he afterwards bitterly regretted—was to import negroes as slaves so as to leave the Indians free. There is no doubt, however, as to the real religious concern of Las Casas. In 1522 he became a Dominican monk, and in 1544, against his will, was made Bishop of Chiapa, a province between Mexico and Honduras. The last twenty years of his long life were spent back in Europe, in ceaseless advocacy of the claims of the Indians.

In 1622, Pope Gregory XV organized the *Sacra Congregatio de Propaganda Fide*, a permanent department of the government of the Church, charged with a three-fold task: to bring into the Roman allegiance the Eastern Christian Churches, to win back Protestant lands, and to convert the heathen. It was a bold and comprehensive aim. The reply of the Reformed Churches was feeble and ineffective till the end of the eighteenth century, but when they did at length awaken to their responsibilities, the memory of Xavier and his successors was a constant spur.

III

Until well on in the eighteenth century, the Protestant Churches remained largely unaware of what had happened both in the geographical and the religious realms. Moreover, the second point made by Dr Latourette in his discussion of the failure of early Protestantism to be missionary-minded is, perhaps, even more important than his brief mention of it suggests. Several of the Reformers held views regarding history and providence which completely excluded any idea of obligation to evangelize other nations and races. Their attitude is well summed up by Dr Findlay:

" Partly in ignorance, and partly in defiance of the facts, Protestant divines asserted that the apostles had already carried the Gospel to all the various lands of the earth—even to America and the Far East! Else how could it be said, ' Their sound went out into all the earth, and their words to the end of the world ' (*Rom*. x. 18)? The nations now Muhammadan or pagan, they inclined to think, were such as had, under one dispensation or another, rejected the light of revealed truth and sinned away their day of grace. ' The holy things of God,' said the Lutheran doctor, Ursinus of Ratisbon, in his reply to Weltz, ' are not to be cast before such dogs and swine! ' The apostolic mandate was addressed, as they argued, to the apostolic age, when it had been duly fulfilled; and the promises of the New Testament concerning ' the Gentiles ' belong to those nations which received and held fast the Gospel, and are now found within the Christian pale."[1]

Further, we have to bear in mind that Luther and Melanchthon expected the end of the Gospel dispensation to come about the middle of the sixteenth century. Large-scale and distant evangelistic enterprises were far from their minds.[2] " It is my firm belief ", said Luther, " that the angels are getting ready, putting on their armour and girding their swords about them, for

[1] Findlay, i. p. 25.
[2] See Dorner, *History of Protestant Theology*, ii. p. 170; Harnack, *History of Dogma*, vii. p. 191.

the last day is already breaking, and the angels are preparing for the battle, when they will overthrow the Turks and hurl them along with the Pope, to the bottom of hell. The world will shortly perish."[1]

Calvin had little or nothing to say of this, but his doctrine of election and predestination, whilst not incompatible with evangelism at home and abroad— as was later to appear—did not initially favour it.

There was, of course, happily, a more attractive Protestant tradition than this. The great Humanist, Erasmus, in his famous *Treatise on Preaching* (1535), had made an eloquent appeal to his contemporaries to carry to Asia and Africa " the wisdom of Christ, more precious than gold, and the pearl of the Gospel, which would put to shame all earthly riches." Justinian von Weltz, mentioned above, was an Austrian baron of the seventeenth century, who, in spite of the contemptuous official attitude of the Lutheran leaders, died as a solitary missionary in Dutch Guiana. There were other individual attempts to carry on the missionary work which had been the glory of earlier ages of the Church's history. In the middle of the sixteenth century the fine-spirited Huguenot, Admiral Coligny, obtained from Calvin a small band of preachers, and sent them to Brazil in connection with a projected French colony there, but the whole venture ended in disaster. Shortly afterwards, under the patronage of Gustavus Vasa, the Scandinavian Churches sought the conversion of Laplanders and Greenlanders; but the motive was Government policy rather than spiritual concern, and there was little success.

[1] H. T. Kerr, *A Compend of Luther's Theology*, p. 244. But note Luther's preface to the German Mass (Kidd, *Documents of the Continental Reformation*, p. 195) and Karl Holl, *Gesammelte Aufsätze*, iii. No. 11, " Luther und die Mission."

In the seventeenth century there was for some years a small missionary college at Leyden from which men were sent to the new Dutch colonies in the East Indies. Among the Leyden professors was Adrianus Savaria, who later became Dean of Westminster. He maintained that " the command to preach the Gospel to all nations binds the Church for all time," though his views were sharply repudiated by Theodore Beza, of Geneva. It was for the missionary chaplains from Leyden that the great lawyer Grotius wrote his famous Latin tract *On the Truth of the Christian Religion* (1627), the germ of which is said to have been composed in vernacular verse, that it might be committed to memory by Dutch sailors and traders, and by them employed, as occasion served, for the propagation of the faith![1] The Dutch Government, however, made the profession of Christianity a condition of civil rights, with most unfortunate consequences. Coercion and political pressure led to a nominal change of religious allegiance by whole populations.

IV

The English colonization of America began in 1578, when at the instigation of Sir Walter Raleigh Queen Elizabeth I gave to Sir Humphrey Gilbert *Letters Patent* " for the inhabiting and planting of our people in America." Richard Hakluyt, in the course of a prospectus, suggested that " this westerne discoverie will be greatly for the inlargement of the gospill of Christe, whereunto the princes of the refourmed relligion are chiefly bounde, amongst whom her majestie ys principall."[2] He cited the work of Roman missionaries

---

[1] *Encyclopædia of Religion and Ethics*, vi. p. 441. Cf. the methods of Las Casas and Xavier.

[2] Quoted by W. L. Sperry, *Religion in America*, 1945, p. 27.

in the Caribbean and elsewhere, but the early settlers were too busy making and defending their homes to give much thought to the Indians whom they drove out. The Pilgrim Fathers, who left Holland and England early in the seventeenth century, had, said one of the first American historians, " an ardent, noble and godly desire, of laying a foundation for spreading the religion of Jesus over the remote regions of the earth."[1] Robert Cushman, in an essay on " The Lawfulness of Plantations," which appeared as early as 1622, urged that it was the duty of colonists to go to the Indians and convert them. The Indians, however, strenuously resisted the new arrivals and the difficulty of establishing friendly relations with them soon caused many of the hard-pressed Puritan settlers to adopt the general attitude of the Reformers to heathen races. They were " Canaanites," and Scripture justified their ruthless extermination. The chequered story of the relations between the colonists and the Indians during the seventeenth century is a sorry one, redeemed only by the few pages which tell of the Christian integrity, heroism and persistence of a small number of individuals and communities.

Roger Williams, who, in 1636, founded the famous Rhode Island Colony on the principle of complete religious freedom, has it to his credit that all his life he was scrupulous in his dealings with the Indians, and that he learned their language and preached to them. It was, however, John Eliot, who gave half a century of devoted service on their behalf, who is rightly honoured as " the apostle of the Indians."

A Cambridge graduate, he had emigrated in 1631 as a young man of twenty-seven, and within a few years of

[1] William Gordon, *History of the American Revolution*, 1788. pp. 7-8.

his arrival in America gave himself with great zeal and wisdom to the conversion of the Massachusetts tribes. " Prayer and pains, through faith in Jesus Christ, will do anything," he once said. Townships of " Praying Indians " were formed, and Eliot built up in time a Christian community numbering three or four thousand Indians. He accomplished the remarkable feat of translating the Bible into the Mohican dialect, and also gave his friends a version of Richard Baxter's *Call to the Unconverted* within a few years of its first appearance in England. It was knowledge of what Eliot was doing which inspired Cromwell in 1648 to persuade the English Parliament to vote a considerable sum of money for an extensive plan of missionary work abroad—a plan set aside, like much else, at the time of the Restoration. In 1649, a Society for the Propagation of the Gospel in New England was established, and a collection made throughout this country which, invested in land, produced a yearly income of some £600, from which grants were made to Eliot and others.[1] When he died in 1690 Eliot was eighty-six years old. Almost all his work was speedily swept away by the wars between the Indians and the colonists, but the knowledge of what he had done remained to challenge subsequent generations, and it was the inspiration of many of the later attempts of S.P.G. chaplains to evangelize the tribes.

Since the late eighteenth century the name of Eliot has been almost always linked with that of Brainerd. With the latter we come to a less shadowy figure, and one whose influence on the Napoleonic generation was

[1] The Society continues in existence in the form of a company, making grants from the income on its investments. For some local details of the Government collection in 1653 see *Historical Sketches of Nonconformity in Cheshire*, 1864, p. 210.

wide and intense. Eliot they could only dimly discern across the mists of more than a century; Brainerd had died but fourteen years before Carey's birth. His was a memorable story. His work among the Indians had lasted only three years, and he died of hereditary consumption at the age of twenty-nine. He had spent himself in such fashion, however, that a considerable body of converted Indians were brought from the New Jersey and Delaware regions and planted on an agricultural settlement. Moreover, Brainerd's *Diary* and *Journal* revealed his day-by-day activities and his most intimate spiritual strivings, and in a way that spoke powerfully to the evangelicals of the late eighteenth century. These writings were published by the great Jonathan Edwards, of New England, to whose daughter, Jerusha, David Brainerd had been deeply attached, though he felt bound to surrender her for the sake of the " enlargement of Christ's Kingdom."

William James described Brainerd as " that genuine saint."[1] A modern editor of the *Diary* and *Journal* has suggested that the secret of the power of his deeds and words lay in his insistence that the inner life is of more importance than the outer, that our experiences here are but a brief probation that may be at any moment ended, and that we are called to unflagging, self-sacrificing diligence and to constant prayer. The distinguishing mark of Brainerd's saintliness is held to be the height and sublimity of his love of God, and the stateliness, austerity almost, that showed itself in his life.[2] " To believe, to suffer, to love," was his motto.

These qualities made an immediate appeal to the promoters of the new missionary societies and to those

[1] *Varieties of Religious Experience*, p. 212.
[2] Dr Alexander Smellie, 1902 edition.

who first went abroad under their auspices. Brainerd's pages do not yield milk for babes; there is too much introspection and often melancholy hanging over them. But for men of spiritual maturity facing heavy odds they are fit food.

There is clear evidence in the *Enquiry* of how, as a young man, William Carey kindled to Brainerd's story. John Ryland described it as " almost a second Bible to him." Carey read it again and again during his difficult early years in India, for it was from its pages that he soonest " caught fire." When the famous Covenant was drafted at Serampore—the basis of the missionary settlement there and at the other stations of the Baptist Missionary Society—it contained these words: " Let us often look at Brainerd in the woods of America, pouring out his very soul before God for the people. Prayer, secret, fervent, expectant, lies at the root of all personal godliness. A competent knowledge of the languages current where a missionary lives, a mild and winning temper, and a heart given up to God— these are the attainments which, more than all other gifts, will fit us to become God's instruments in the great work of human redemption." It was to Brainerd that Henry Martyn looked for much of his inspiration, and their lives present not a few striking parallels. Martyn was probably introduced to Brainerd's story by Charles Simeon of Cambridge, as was his undergraduate contemporary Samuel Marsden, who went to Australia as chaplain to a party of convicts, spending himself during more than forty stormy years for the people of New South Wales and the Maoris of New Zealand. These devoted men, like many who have succeeded them, kindled and rekindled their spirits at Brainerd's steady and intense flame.

V

Brainerd received grants for his work among the American Indians from a small Scottish Society for the Propagation of Christian Knowledge. It had been formed in 1709 on the analogy of the two great societies which came into existence in London in the closing years of the reign of William III—the Society for Promoting Christian Knowledge (1698-9) and the Society for the Propagation of the Gospel in Foreign Parts (1701). Both these bodies can now look back on a continuous history of nearly two and a half centuries, during which valuable work has been done for the extension and building up of the Church overseas. They may justly be proud of the fact that, in the years before Christian people generally had been roused to their missionary obligations, they made noble attempts to help in the evangelization of those of other races and nations. Theirs was indeed an essential part in the preparation of the Church for what was to come, and they shared in due course in the outburst of new life which came in the Napoleonic era.

In the founding both of the S.P.C.K. and the S.P.G. Thomas Bray was the leading figure. He was Rector of Sheldon, in Warwickshire, and in 1696 was appointed Ecclesiastical Commissary for Maryland by the Bishop of London, who, there being at the time no colonial Anglican bishops, was supposed to add the oversight of the American settlements to his other duties. There were, as a matter of fact, very few clergy of the Church of England in the American colonies. In preparation for a personal visit to Maryland, Bray endeavoured to recruit some more men and to furnish them with libraries. It was out of these and other beneficent

activites in which he engaged that the earlier of the two
societies came, its aim being the spread of Christian
knowledge at home and in the plantations and colonies
of the New World by means of libraries and charity
schools. Four lay friends were associated with Bray in
this first venture. His visit to Maryland quickened his
zeal, and soon after his return to England the S.P.G.
was formed. The " foreign parts," which its title had in
view, were the colonies and dependencies of Britain and
her " factories beyond the seas."[1] Their spiritual welfare
was to be its concern, and its main line of activity was
to be the providing of official chaplains " for the
instruction of the King's loving subjects in the Christian
religion " and the winning to the Christian faith of the
aborigines and the negro slaves. Till his death in 1730,
Bray remained active in these and many other enterprises, making on their behalf plain, forcible and racy
appeals—" a striking instance," as Overton observes,
" of what a man may effect without any extraordinary
genius and without special influence."[2]

It is the S.P.G. which first concerns us here. It began
its work with zeal and earnestness. Not only were
additional chaplains found for the colonists, but as early
as 1704 a grant was made for a school for negro slaves in
New York, of which the headmaster was a French
Protestant. In the same year the first missionary to the
Indians was appointed, Thoroughgood Moore. He
made his way to Albany, then a frontier town on the
edge of the territory of the Mohawks. In less than
twleve months Moore had decided that he was not the
man for the task, and the subsequent years provide a

---

[1] As early as 1703 books, including " Greek liturgies and Testaments,"
were supplied to the English merchants in Russia.

[2] *Dictionary of National Biography*, ii. p. 1148. Cf. J. W. Lyddeker,
*Thomas Bray, Founder of Missionary Enterprise*, 1944.

very chequered story of intermittent missionary activity, few men staying long enough to do much effective work and the fact that they were backed by the British garrisons being usually more of a hindrance than a help. French intrigues during the struggle for Canada further complicated the situation. Then came the revolt of the colonies and the War of American Independence. The resources of the S.P.G. were never very large in the eighteenth century—fluctuating between £2,000 and £3,000 per annum—and there were many demands to be met. In consequence there was never very vigorous prosecution of missionary work among the Indians. Yet there were fine figures among the missionary chaplains. Of those who worked among the Mohawks, Henry Barclay, John Ogilvie and John Stuart deserve mention, and all three were born in America, coming to England for ordination. Their influence can be traced on the strong and gifted succession of Mohawk chieftains. Stuart came of Scottish Covenanting stock and was a fine figure of a man, six feet four inches tall; he was kept a prisoner for three years by the American " rebels " and suffered many hardships, but lived to earn the proud title of " the Father of the Church of England in Canada."[1]

South Carolina, New York, New England, New Jersey, Pennsylvania, Virginia, Maryland, Newfoundland, North Carolina, the Windward Islands, Nova Scotia, Georgia, the Bahamas, the Mosquito Coast of Central America, West Africa, Quebec, New Brunswick, Ontario, Cape Breton—to all these places S.P.G. chaplains were appointed prior to 1792. In most of them there were negro slaves, and little

---

[1] For the preceding paragraph see the fine historical study, by J. W. Lydekker, *The Faithful Mohawks.* C.U.P., 1938.

communities of baptized negroes were soon to be found in amongst their white brethren. The bequest of the scholarly Christopher Codrington, formerly Captain-General and Commander-in-Chief of the Leeward Islands, gave the S.P.G. in 1712 two slave-plantations in Barbados for the foundation of a college in which professors and pupils were to be under vows of poverty, chastity and obedience. They were to study medicine and divinity " that by the apparent usefulness of the former to all mankind they may both endear themselves to the people, and have the better opportunities of doing good to men's souls, whilst they are taking care of their bodies." The monastic intention of the benefactor was not carried out, but Codrington College was built and still continues its usefulness. When the emancipation movement gathered strength the slave-plantations became something of an embarrassment. The S.P.G. clung to the old order, and it could rightly point to much that had been done for the negroes.

The work on the west coast of Africa deserves more than a bare mention. Thomas Thompson, a former Fellow of Christ's College, Cambridge, had given five years of zealous chaplaincy service in New Jersey, making a number of fruitful contacts with the negroes. In 1751 he persuaded the S.P.G. to appoint him as a missionary to the Africans of the Gold Coast.

" In an ordinary way one Labourer can do but little," he wrote, " yet . . . no doubt it must be of divine Grace that the Conversion of that People is wrought, whether it be by many or by few; but if ever a Church is founded among them, some Body must lay the first Stone . . . and should I be prevented in my Intention, God only knows how long it may be before any other Person will take the same Resolution."[1]

After four years of varied activity there, during which he made a number of journeys into the interior, Thompson's health broke down, but not before he had sent to England three young African boys to be trained at the expense of the S.P.G. as missionaries to their countrymen. One of these boys, Philip Quaque, became the first of any non-European race since the Reformation to receive Anglican ordination, and, returning to the Gold Coast, he continued in the service of the S.P.G., though without much fruit for his labours, till his death in 1816.

On the whole it is clear that the S.P.G. could not prosecute its wider missionary purpose with sufficient freedom, energy or adaptability to achieve great success, or to make a very deep impression on the Christian conscience. Melvill Horne, in his 1794 *Letters*, is very scathing and calls attention to a number of abuses. Perhaps the experience of the most famous S.P.G. chaplain of the eighteenth century may be taken as a parable. It was the S.P.G. which, in 1735, sent John Wesley to Georgia. He was then intending to give his life to the evangelization of the American Indians. God had other plans for him. He had first to be taught the inadequacy of his own spiritual resources. But, as Dr Findlay well puts it, " his whole subsequent thinking and teaching were coloured, and the trend of his work for his own country influenced, by the two years of early manhood spent on the edge of the pagan world."[2] It was not until the revival had brought new life to the English Churches that they could successfully

[1] *S.P.G. Journal*, xi. p. 309. See the interesting facsimile reproduction, *An Account of Two Missionary Voyages*, by Thomas Thompson, A.M. S.P.G., 1937.     [2] Findlay, i. p. 30.

undertake the evangelization of the non-Christian world, but the contacts which the S.P.G. had had with Indians and negroes permanently influenced what was later attempted.

## VI

The S.P.C.K., the older of Thomas Bray's societies, found many channels of service, and it is its great glory that in the eighteenth century it gave substantial aid to the missionary work in India undertaken by what is usually styled the Danish-Halle Mission. Here we come on an enterprise notable in itself, of outstanding importance for the modern beginnings of the Christian Church in India, and of no small influence on the missionary developments of Napoleonic times.

In the early years of the eighteenth century, King Frederick Christian IV of Denmark, himself no saint, became concerned for the spiritual condition of his non-Christian subjects in India and in Greenland. No one could be found in Denmark itself to undertake missions, but the court chaplain discovered in Germany two scholarly young men, who had been students at Halle in the university recently established under the influence of Spener, " the Father of Pietism." The young men wanted to be missionaries, though they had not known where they would be able to go. Pietism placed renewed emphasis on Bible study, personal devotion and the practical expression of the Christian faith, and at Halle A. H. Francke fired many men with enthusiasm for work overseas. Ziegenbalg and Plütschau were duly commissioned by the Danish King. They reached the little dominion of Tranquebar, on the east coast of India south of Madras, in 1705, and there began a noble tradition, which for ninety years remained the only

Protestant missionary enterprise in the land, and which, though it compromised in regard to caste, was most fruitful in preparing the way for later developments. Queen Anne's husband had a German chaplain[1] who early became interested in the venture, and he tried to secure aid for it from the recently formed S.P.G. This society, however, as already noted, had decided to restrict its interpretation of " foreign parts " to British dominions. The request was, therefore, passed on to the S.P.C.K., who worthily responded to it.

Ziegenbalg translated into Tamil the whole of the New Testament and much of the Old. When he died in 1719, in spite of much indifference and opposition a number of converts had been won. A little stream of missionary recruits came out from Halle to continue the work, among them Christian Friedrich Schwartz, a man of apostolic simplicity and zeal, who from 1750 till his death in 1798 laboured " almost without rest " all along the coast from Madras in the north to Ceylon in the south. He became known as " the priest-king of Tanjore," and by his transparent goodness exercised a remarkable influence on all who came in contact with him. " Send me the Christian," cried the fierce adventurer Hyder Ali on one occasion, " I can trust him."

In the earliest years of the Danish-Halle Mission, Susanna Wesley, in the Epworth Rectory, read an account of the work of Ziegenbalg and Plütschau. " For several days," she said, " I could think or speak of little else." She resolved to give a weekly missionary lesson to her children, and the great John always recognized how much he owed to this. When Thomas

[1] A. W. Boehme, himself a Pietist. See J. Rieger in *And Other Pastors of Thy Flock*, 1942, pp. 105 f.

Coke corresponded with Charles Grant in 1786 about the possibility of a mission in Bengal, he urged that it would be " very expedient that our missionaries should visit the settlements of the Danish Mission," and Charles Grant would certainly have agreed, for it was a meeting with Schwartz at Madras, in 1773, that had first kindled missionary fire in the heart of the then young servant of the East India Company. Carey knew of the work at Tranquebar, and alluded to it in the *Enquiry*. Some time after his arrival in Bengal, he wrote to " the venerable Mr Schwartz." The letter arrived when the saintly German was on his death-bed, but it was read to him, and a younger colleague replied on his behalf. Carey had characteristically asked as to " the inward religion of the heart among the converted heathens," and was told that, as he lay dying, Schwartz had said regarding the Christians of Tanjore: " There is in all a good beginning. If another says, ' But there is nothing perfect '; let him examine himself and then judge."[1]

There were then nine missionaries on the Tranquebar coast. Not many months after Carey received the answer to his letter, a bewildered and harassed party of Baptist missionaries sought asylum from the hostility of the East India Company at the Danish settlement of Serampore, in Bengal. The Governor admitted and protected them. He had known Schwartz.

VII

The influence of Xavier, Eliot and Brainerd on those who awakened the Churches at the end of the eighteenth century was the intimate touch of one loving

[1] Carey's biographers do not seem to have called attention to this correspondence, but the details and the letters will be found in *The Periodical Accounts of the B.M.S.*, i. pp. 398, 421, 428-33.

heart upon another. The S.P.G. chaplaincy tradition and the Danish-Halle Mission showed notable successions of men giving themselves to the task of evangelism. But here again it was individuals who were involved, and no large number of them. We have now to consider the work of the Moravians—perhaps the greatest single influence in the rekindling of the missionary purpose of the Christian Church.

It had its link with the story just told. In 1715, Ziegenbalg came back from Tranquebar for a brief visit to Europe. Among those who heard him, when he came to Francke's home in Halle, was the schoolboy, Zinzendorf, who had already resolved to give his life to Christian evangelism. It was to his estate that there came, seven years later, seeking protection and freedom, some humble families from Moravia, who cherished the old Bible-loving tradition of the Church of the Brethren, the *Unitas Fratrum*. There in Saxony, with Zinzendorf's help, they built the township of Herrnhut, and in 1727 were made conscious that they were to be called by the Spirit of God to important new service. Zinzendorf took certain of them with him to Copenhagen for the coronation of King Frederick IV's successor, and there they came to know a West Indian slave, brought from the island of St Thomas by a Danish nobleman, and two Greenland Eskimos. The stories they told led to one and another from Herrnhut desiring to go as missionary-settlers among these distant and needy peoples.

A beginning was made in August 1732, when a potter and a carpenter set off for St Thomas. They had but a few shillings in their pockets, and they travelled on foot to Copenhagen. The potter was ready, if necessary, to become a slave, that he might work among the negroes.

Five months later, two more of the brotherhood set out
for Greenland, and from then onwards a steady stream
of these devout men made their way to different parts of
the world " to win for the Lamb that was slain the
reward of His sufferings." They showed amazing
heroism, persistence and single-mindedness, and their
hardships were shared by women as devoted as themselves, the New Testament phrase " two by two " being
interpreted as meaning man and wife. Within fifteen
years there were sixteen different mission-fields, and the
Gospel was being proclaimed by Moravians to negroes,
Hottentots, Eskimos, Greenlanders and American
Indians. It swiftly became an international movement,
the missionary ranks including Germans, Dutch,
British and Americans. " In two decades," says
Warneck, " the little Church of the Brethren called
more missions into life than did the whole of Protestantism in two centuries."

Their contemporaries, as they came to hear of what
was taking place, were many of them deeply stirred.
There was a party of Moravians on the boat which took
John Wesley to Georgia in 1735, and in the next few
years the young " Methodist " owed much to their
influence. Shortly after his conversion in 1738 he visited
Herrnhut. Methodism, it has been said, stands in
almost a filial relation to Moravianism. On Carey
the whole movement had a profound effect. " Have
not the missionaries of the *Unitas Fratrum* encountered
the scorching heat of Abyssinia and the frozen climes of
Greenland and Labrador, their difficult languages and
savage manners? " he asks in the *Enquiry*. " None of
the moderns have equalled the Moravian Brethren in
this good work." At the meeting in Kettering in 1792,
at which the Baptist Missionary Society was formed, to

enforce his pleas he drew from his pocket a copy of the latest *Periodical Accounts* of the Moravian missions. Money was voted to the Moravians for their work by the infant B.M.S., and when at length Carey got to Serampore the missionary settlement there was modelled on the Moravian pattern. The other societies were also much influenced. The famous preacher, Rowland Hill, for example, a leader in the founding of both the London Missionary Society and the Religious Tract Society, had for many years taken a deep interest in the remarkably successful work done by the Moravian, Peter Brown, in Antigua.[1] A man of simple heart, Brown was " always with the slaves in their free time and often ate out of their calabashes,"[2] and he saw the number of baptized Christians increase from fourteen, when he arrived in the island in 1769, to 7,400 at the time of his death in 1791

Melvill Horne was eloquent in his praise. " The Moravians have been among us what the Jesuits were in the Roman Church," he declared. " They have laboured, and suffered, and effected more than all of us."[3] The secret he believed to be the fact that their missionaries were men of ardent personal piety, volunteers, and at work in groups. Even more striking was Wilberforce's tribute in his *Practical View*. After admitting the obvious dangers implicit in Moravian language about the guidance of the Holy Spirit, he says that they " have perhaps excelled all mankind in solid and unequivocal proofs of the love of Christ, and of the most ardent, and active, and patient zeal in His service. It is a zeal tempered with prudence, softened with

[1] Edwin Sidney, *The Life of the Rev. Rowland Hill*, 1834, pp. 152 f.
[2] Quoted in *The Advance Guard: Two Hundred Years of Moravian Missions*, 1932, p. 26.     [3] *Letters on Missions*, p. 34.

meekness, soberly aiming at great ends by the gradual
operation of well-adapted means, supported by a
courage which no danger can intimidate and a quiet
constancy which no hardships can exhaust."

"Here," declares Dr Latourette, "was a new
phenomenon in the expansion of Christianity, an entire
community, of families as well as of the unmarried,
devoted to the propagation of the faith."[1]

[1] *A History of the Expansion of Christianity*, iii. p. 47.

# CHAPTER III

# THE MISSIONARY AWAKENING

" Surely a Society might be formed for the purpose;
and if for Wales, why not for the Kingdom: why
not for the whole world ?" Joseph Hughes, 1802.

I

THOSE MENTIONED in the previous chapter lived in the
period from 1500-1750, which Dr Latourette describes
as one of advance in the fortunes of Christianity. Most
of the progress was made by the Roman Church. That
of Protestants was much slighter and more sporadic.
From 1750-1815 there came what he calls " not so
much a recession as a pause " during which " Christianity was gathering momentum for another advance." It
was in truth a notable period, for if we extend it by
another ten years it saw the establishment of missionary
societies in all the main non-Roman Churches of
Europe and America. Protestantism began at length to
awake to its missionary obligations and opportunities.

The first moves were somewhat hesitant and tentative. Challenged by the Danish-Halle Mission, and the
missionary activity of the Moravians, Philip Doddridge,
the well-known Independent minister and hymn-writer,
pleaded in 1741 for the establishment of missionary
societies within local Churches. His scheme met with
no success. When he read the life of Brainerd his
eagerness increased and he tried to interest some of his
students in going to America to work among the

Indians.  He died, however, in 1751 before anything definite had developed.[1]

The eighteenth-century Dissenters could not remain unaware of the missionary enterprises of others.  They were stirred by what they heard of conditions in the colonies from George Whitefield and some of their own brethren in America.  It was Selina, Countess of Huntingdon who next tried to organize a missionary expedition.[2]

George Whitefield, when he died in 1770, bequeathed to the Countess of Huntingdon an orphanage and estate in Georgia.  Her final breach with the Church of England had not then taken place, and she was busily engaged in assisting evangelical clergymen and Methodists with open-handed charity.  Trevecca College she had but recently established.  In the autumn of 1772 she summoned all her clergy and students to meet there to consider means " of promoting the Knowledge of the Lord, not only in the Provinces of America, but also (by the intended measure) a supply of missions will be provided to carry it into the back settlements and among the heathen nations."  A missionary party was selected, led by a certain Mr Piercy, and charged to reorganize the orphanage, and to engage in a varied programme of activities which included work among both negroes and Red Indians.  The party embarked, amid signs of considerable enthusiasm, at the end of October 1772, after solemn services at Trevecca, at Tottenham Court Chapel and in the open air on Tower Hill, where " an immense concourse of people " is said to have assembled.  Safely arrived in Georgia, the party

[1] See E. A. Payne, " Doddridge and the Missionary Enterprise." *Philip Doddridge* (ed. by G. Nuttall), 1951, ch. IV.

[2] See *The Life and Times of Selina, Countess of Huntingdon*, 1839-40, ii. chs. 40 and 41.

engaged in widespread itinerancy. Many negro converts were made, and most promising contacts were
established with the Cherokee Indians.

The earliest reports caused the indefatigable Countess, who was then sixty-five years old, to write: " Some
great, very great, work is intended by the Lord among
the heathen. Should this appear I should be rejoiced to
go myself to establish a College for the Indian nations."
Unfortunately, a series of misfortunes soon occurred.
The orphanage was destroyed by fire; the Countess and
her agents compromised on the slave issue and engaged
in the trade; the revolt of the colonies disorganized all
the work, and led finally to the seizure of the property;
and the financial transactions of Mr Piercy, chiefly in
the matter of slaves, caused suspicion. In 1784, however, the Countess, whose " chapels " were by then
having to register as dissenting meeting-houses,
appointed a new head of the orphanage, and wrote
letters to George Washington, outlining a plan to convert all the revenues of her American estates into a fund
for the establishment of a mission to the Indians. But
this project also was frustrated by the consequences of
the War of Independence.

The efforts of the Countess failed, but one who had
been in close contact with her played later an important
part in the founding of the London Missionary Society.
Thomas Haweis became one of the chaplains of the
Countess in 1774, and if not himself present at the
Trevecca gathering in 1772, was certainly familiar with
the details of the missionary scheme. In 1787 or 1789
(perhaps a year or so earlier) he discussed with the
Countess, he says, the sending of two of her students to
the South Seas. On her death in 1791 Haweis became
one of her executors. It was his pleas which in 1795

directed the attention of the London Missionary Society to Tahiti. There were obvious similarities between the expedition of the *Duff* in 1796, of which we shall later tell, and that of 1772. So much so that when the *Duff* sailed, the *Evangelical Review* printed some stanzas which the Hon. and Rev. Walter Shirley had composed twenty-four years earlier.

II

We come next to Thomas Coke. He and his work are not easy to classify. He has some claim to be considered the one who in England first awakened his generation to its missionary tasks, for it was in 1784, two years before Carey raised his question in the Northampton Fraternal, that Coke put out his " Plan of the Society for the Establishment of Missions among the Heathen."[1] In 1786, on his second voyage to America, Coke was driven by storms to the Island of Antigua, and there began his afterwards ceaseless labours for the slaves of the West Indies. Coke's work, however, was of a very personal and individualistic kind. In 1794, Melvill Horne could write, not untruly, of what Coke had done for the West Indian islands: " Hitherto those missions may be considered as *his* missions, rather than those of the Methodists."[2] Not till 1804 was a " Committee of Finance and Advice " set up to assist him in his superintendency, and it was then that, according to Dr Findlay, " the work was passing out of the stage of personal adventure into that of organized Church

[1] A. W. Harrison, *The Evangelical Revival and Christian Reunion*, 1942, p. 174, claims that the introduction of Methodism into the West Indies in 1760, into Nova Scotia in 1765 and into the American colonies in 1766 marks the real beginning of Methodist foreign missions.

[2] *Letters on Missions*, p. 136.

direction."[1] The Methodist Missionary Society was not organized until after Coke's death. He seems, therefore, best placed among the forerunners. And a notable one he was.

Born in Brecon—"his Welsh blood was soon up," said Southey—after graduating at Oxford he returned home for a time. His father was a doctor of influence, and young Coke inherited wealth as well as ability. After deciding to enter the Church, he secured a Somersetshire curacy, and there passed from being a rather stiff High Churchman to being an eager evangelical. The spirit of revival was moving through the land, and Coke yielded all his energies and abilities to the new movement. In 1776, being then twenty-nine years old, he met John Wesley, and the two were swiftly drawn into intimate friendship. Some of Coke's parishioners resented his changed style and he was driven to begin preaching in the open air. Before long he left his charge to give all his time to itinerant evangelism. "Brother, go out," said Wesley, "and preach the Gospel to all the world." The Methodist leader had recently begun sending men to the American colonies, first Boardman and Pilmoor, then Asbury and Wright, then Rankin and Shadford. It was to the last of these that Wesley gave the farewell word: "I let you loose, George, on the great continent of America. Publish your message in the open face of the sun, and do all the good you can."

Coke meantime was busy in Ireland, and in his first tentative plans for "Missions among the Heathen." When the War of American Independence ended, leadership was clearly badly needed across the Atlantic, if American Methodists were to maintain their

[1] Findlay, i. p. 36.

organization and their contacts. Wesley decided to appoint Asbury and Coke as " superintendents." It was characteristic of the latter that, before accepting, he took two months to examine the patristic precedents for such an office, recognizing how closely it approximated to that of " bishop." Driven ashore at Antigua, on Christmas Day, 1786, he found himself in touch not only with the *élite* of West Indian planter society, but also with a fine body of Christian negroes, the fruit of the evangelical and social work of the family of the Honourable Nathaniel Gilbert, and of the labours of a group of Moravians, led by Peter Brown. Gilbert was lawyer, planter and slave-owner. In 1758 John Wesley had preached in his home at Wandsworth, and subsequently baptized two of the negroes Gilbert had there as servants. When they returned to Antigua, Gilbert, his wife and his doctor brother did a notable work of religious and social uplift, and he has been called " the father of Methodism in the Western Isles."[1]

From 1786 onwards Coke became an intense missionary enthusiast, ceaselessly active in the West Indian islands and in his appeals for help to the Methodists of Britain and America. Slowly he gathered workers and funds. He took a strong line against slavery, supporting the efforts of the emancipators, and interesting himself in the Sierra Leone Company. He was in touch with Wilberforce, Grant and Hardcastle, and many others whose names are associated with the formation of the missionary societies. Short of stature, with a bright winning countenance, impulsive, not unambitious, but an unselfish worker of generous spirit, in his missionary journeyings "neither zeal nor resource ever failed him."[2]

[1] Findlay, i. p. 32.
[2] *Dictionary of National Biography*, iv. p. 705.

In 1804 Coke secured the appointment of a Methodist at Gibraltar; in 1811 George Warren was sent to West Africa, where earlier unsuccessful attempts had been made. Then, as the support in England for the more than forty Methodist missionaries seemed fairly secure, Coke decided to carry out his long-cherished project of a missionary journey to the East. The new Charter of the East India Company gave permission for missionary work, and Coke had even dreamed of himself as a real bishop in India. He and six other Methodists set out for Ceylon at the end of 1813. The journey round the Cape of Good Hope was a slow one. On May 3rd, 1814, the eloquent and fascinating little doctor was found dead on the floor of his cabin.

His stimulating figure is to be seen coming and going during the missionary plannings which went on throughout the twenty years of the Revolutionary and Napoleonic struggle. What Melvill Horne has to say of Methodists in general fits Thomas Coke admirably, and indicates the characteristic contribution which they, and he with them, made in those stirring days: " The zeal of the Methodist blazes, and burns everything before it," Horne declares. " He is open, active, bold, and ardent. He sees himself in a pushing world, and pushes with the foremost. He cannot brook the general coldness; and, fearless of consequences, censures with severity what he deems censurable. He mixes in the world; makes a hundred different attempts to effect his purpose; and, if baffled in them all, directs his labours to some other quarter, which affords full scope to his activity. He lives in action."[1]

[1] *Letters on Missions*, p. 36.

### III

The distinction of founding the first society deliberately and exclusively aimed at the evangelization of the non-Christian world belongs to an obscure little company of Midland Baptist ministers. Their story will always be an impressive reminder of the truth on which the apostle Paul insisted when writing to his friends in Corinth. " God hath chosen the foolish things of the world to confound the wise; and God hath chosen the weak things of the world to confound the things that are mighty." It was not in London that the first society was formed, nor was it by men of experience, influence, learning or wealth. The home of the Baptist Missionary Society was Kettering, a small Northamptonshire town which had then but three thousand inhabitants; and those who took so notable and daring a step, whilst aware of the powerful new political and religious forces that were at work, stood only on the very fringe of their influence.

" The origin of this Society," said the first secretary, writing in 1795, " will be found in the workings of our Brother Carey's mind." Born in a Northamptonshire hamlet, the son of the parish clerk and schoolmaster, Carey had wished as a lad to be a gardener, but had been driven by ill health to shoemaking. After his conversion, when he was about seventeen and a half— a conversion which took him from the parish church to the formerly despised dissenting chapel—he became a preacher also, settling at length in the village of Moulton. The responsibilities of an increasing family and his own bookish inclinations made him open a small school as well.

Carey's conviction about the missionary obligation

resting upon Christians can be traced back to the year of his baptism as a young man of twenty-two, perhaps behind that event to the very beginnings of personal faith in his heart. His understanding of the way of Christ he ever felt he must share—with his own family and with any in neighbouring Northamptonshire villages who would listen to him. His interest in the world around was extended and deepened by an uncle who had fought in Canada, and by his love of reading, and this must have predisposed him to give a wide interpretation of the familiar words of the Gospel. The more he studied the Bible, wrestling with it in Hebrew and Greek, which he had learned with practically no assistance, the more sure he became that the commands of Christ were being inadequately fulfilled. Carey had perhaps heard Wesley preach at Whittlebury; he had some contact with Thomas Scott, then a curate in the neighbourhood and but recently come under the influence of John Newton; he must have known something of the movement which we now call the Evangelical Revival. But to a large extent we see in Carey an independent mind working out its own slow but sure conclusions. " He seems to have been," says Latourette, " the first Anglo-Saxon Protestant either in America or in Great Britain to propose that Christians take concrete steps to bring their Gospel to all the human race."[1]

He owed not a little to his friends among the Northamptonshire Baptist ministers, and notably to vigorous Andrew Fuller, who had thrown off the fetters of a high and narrow Calvinism, to learned John Ryland, and to cautious, kindly John Sutcliff. It was the last of these who, when he discovered what had been happening in New England and read something of the story of the

[1] Latourette, op. cit., iv. p. 68.

"Great Awakening" there, called the Northamptonshire Baptist churches to special prayer for an outpouring of the Spirit of God. It was probably these prayer meetings, as much as any other single influence, which prepared the little group of ministers to venture on the formation of a missionary society.[1]

For some time they hesitated. The older generation was frankly impatient and sceptical. But Carey was not to be turned aside. Rebuffed in 1786, he persisted in his pleas, struggled with the preparation of the *Enquiry*, slowly convinced his friends that something must be done, endured many setbacks and disappointments, but at last had his chance when his turn came to preach to the Northamptonshire Baptist Association at Whitsuntide, 1792. Some twenty Baptist churches were there represented, covering the East Midland counties from Hertfordshire up to Lincolnshire. Carey himself was by then minister of a church in Leicester, and the gatherings were being held in Nottingham. Even so, he can have had no very large or influential congregation; but he poured out to them his soul under the famous phrases—" Expect great things from God—Attempt great things for God." There is no doubt as to the impression made by the sermon, but there was still reluctance to do anything definite about the matter. What could such a company expect to do? The ministers were more interested in the beginnings of the struggle against the slave trade and in the news about the French Revolution. " Is there nothing again going to be done, sir?" cried Carey afterwards to his friend Fuller. And at the very last moment, before the company dispersed, it was " Resolved, that a plan be

[1] See E. A. Payne, *The Prayer Call of 1784*. Baptist Laymen's Movement, 1941.

prepared against the next Ministers' Meeting at Kettering, for forming a Baptist Society for propagating the Gospel among the Heathens."

So it came about that, on October 2nd, 1792, in the little back parlour of a house in Kettering, the Baptist Missionary Society was formed. There were fourteen people present—one of them a Kettering wool stapler, who was probably acting as host, one a young ministerial student from Bristol, the others Baptist pastors, most of them with the slenderest resources and little knowledge of the ways of the world. They had no clear plans as to how missionaries could be obtained, or where they could be sent. The decision once taken, however, events soon directed them onwards. A ship's surgeon, who had been in Bengal, was introduced to them, and persuaded Carey to offer to go back to India with him. It was a tremendous venture for a married man of over thirty with three young sons and a reluctant wife, but Carey knew that he must back his own words at whatever cost.

There were not a few delays and embarrassments before Carey and his strange companion, Thomas, sailed for Bengal. But with the meeting at Kettering and the sending out of Carey and Thomas a beginning had been made, and within a few months it was clear that there were to be repercussions throughout the whole Christian Church.

IV

The quarter of a century which followed 1792 saw the establishment of an extraordinary number of religious and philanthropic societies, among them most of the larger and better-known missionary bodies of this country, America and the Continent of Europe. A mere list of names is impressive and it could be considerably lengthened.

1792. The Particular Baptist Society for the Propagation of the Gospel amongst the Heathen (B.M S.).

1795. The Missionary Society (L.M.S.).

1796. The Society for Bettering the Condition of the Poor.

The Edinburgh and Glasgow Missionary Societies.

1797. The Netherlands Missionary Society.

The Baptist Itinerant Society (later Baptist Home Missionary Society).

1799. The Society for Missions to Africa and the East (C.M.S.).

The Religious Tract Society (R.T.S., now incorporated in the United Society for Christian Literature).

1802. The Society for the Suppression of Vice (succeeding Wilberforce's "Proclamation Society" of 1787).

1803. The Sunday School Union (succeeding the Sunday School Society of 1785).

1804. The British and Foreign Bible Society.

1807. The African Institution (succeeding the Sierra Leone Company).

1808. The Royal Lancasterian Society (later the British and Foreign School Society).

1809. The National Society for Promoting the Education of the Poor in the principles of the Established Church throughout England and Wales.

The London Society for the Propagation of the Gospel amongst the Jews.

1810. The American Board of Commissioners for Foreign Missions.

1813-18. The Wesleyan Methodist Missionary Society.

1814. The American Baptist Missionary Union.

1815. The Basel Evangelical Missionary Society.

1816. The American Bible Society.
The General Baptist Missionary Society.
The Society for the Reformation of Prison Discipline.

1819. The Missionary Society of the Methodist Episcopal Church.

1821. The Domestic and Foreign Missionary Society of the Protestant Episcopal Church of the U.S.A.

1822. The Paris Society for Evangelical Missions.

1823. Colonial and Continental Church Society.

1824. The Committee for Foreign Missions of the General Assembly of the Church of Scotland.

Some of the names are cumbrous and raise a smile today. Can any other period, however, show anything to compare with this amazing outburst of zeal and enthusiasm? As one studies the list and learns something of the origin of these societies, a number of significant facts emerge. It was the twenty years from 1795 to 1815 that proved specially prolific of these new organizations, that is, the period of Napoleon's rise to power and final downfall. It was in 1795 that the young Corsican General of Artillery, after quelling a reactionary rising in Paris, was made General of the Interior. In 1799 he became First Consul, and in 1804 the title Emperor of the French was conferred upon him. The year 1814 saw his enforced abdication, and the following year his final banishment to St Helena. It was, therefore, in the period of tense struggle, with the final issue often in doubt, that most of these societies were formed.

Many of them were very closely linked together, and their stories lead on from one to another. For example, Carey's first letter from India played an important part in the starting of " The Missionary Society," the organization now known as the L.M.S. Carey's friend, John Ryland, had moved to Bristol. When he received the letter in July 1794 he invited a group of acquaintances to hear it read. One of them brought with him David Bogue, a licensed preacher of the Church of Scotland, who since 1777 had been in charge of the Congregational church in Gosport. Bogue was deeply moved and at once drafted an appeal " To the Evangelical Dissenters who practise Infant Baptism," which appeared in the *Evangelical Magazine* in September. Two months later, Dr Thomas Haweis, who had been at one time curate at St Mary's, Oxford, and then, through his friendship with the early Methodists, became trustee and executor of the Countess of Huntingdon, published in the same periodical a lengthy review of Melvill Horne's *Letters on Missions*, which were the result of the author's experiences as a chaplain in Sierra Leone. These two articles fired the enthusiasm of the editor, John Eyre,[1] and he, David Bogue and Thomas Haweis were outstanding among the group which, in September 1795, amid considerable popular excitement, formed the new Society whose " sole object " was stated to be " to spread the knowledge of Christ among heathen and other unenlightened nations," and which was from the first on a broad interdenominational basis. The first B.M.S. collection

---

[1] A Devonshire youth, trained at the Countess of Huntingdon's College at Trevecca, he had in 1779 taken orders in the Church of England.

of gifts and promises at the Kettering meeting had yielded £13 2s. 6d., a wonderfully generous response considering the slender resources of those present. On the evening before the L.M.S. was formally constituted in the old Spa Fields chapel, a subscription list was opened, and it was recorded that " the liberal contributions and annual subscriptions of that evening sufficiently demonstrated that this excellent cause would never fail for want of pecuniary assistance."

The influence of Carey can also be traced on the men who founded the Church Missionary Society. Charles Simeon, the famous evangelical clergyman of Cambridge, became an eager reader of the *Periodical Accounts* issued by the B.M.S., and made known their contents to his undergraduate friends. The same publication was studied by several members of the Clapham Sect, and helped to deepen their feeling that Carey had been right when he said in the *Enquiry* that " in the present divided state of Christendom, it would be more likely for good to be done by each denomination engaging separately in the work, than if they were to embark on it conjointly." The broad constitution of the L.M.S. was excellent from many points of view, but some felt unable to co-operate with it, particularly those in responsible positions in the Church of England, and so at length, though not without hesitation and the overcoming of some opposition, there was formed by Simeon, John Venn and other evangelical churchmen " The Society for Missions to Africa and the East,"[1] which had episcopal order as one of the main planks in its platform.

---

[1] This title was apparently never widely used. " The Missions Society " or " The Society for Missions," as it was colloquially known, adopted in 1812 its present official title " The Church Missionary Society for Africa and the East."

Within a month of the founding of the C.M.S., in 1799, the Religious Tract Society was started, and its leaders were drawn from those already deeply engaged with the L.M.S. and the C.M.S. It was very largely the same group of men who five years later, in 1804, became the founders of the Bible Society. The Netherlands Missionary Society had already been formed to assist the L.M.S., and the Society for the Propagation of the Gospel Amongst the Jews was also at first very closely connected with it. The zeal of the supporters of " The Missionary Society " knew indeed no bounds. " The L.M.S. are forming committees of two or three of their friends," wrote Dr Thomas Coke, the Methodist, in October 1812, " to raise annual subscriptions among our Societies and hearers for the support of *their* missions." This undoubtedly stimulated the Methodists to the organization of their own missionary society.

In America, in 1810, Adoniram Judson and three fellow-students from the Andover Theological Institution, desiring to serve overseas, wrote offering themselves to the L.M.S. Before any definite arrangements had been made, however, they succeeded in getting the American Board of Commissioners for Foreign Missions set up. Judson and Rice, when they reached India, became Baptists, and then, partly at Carey's instigation, the American Baptist Missionary Union was established for their support.

Thomas Chalmers, who became one of the most important members of the first missionary committee of the Scottish Church, was deeply influenced by Wilberforce, by the Baptist pioneers and by what he knew of the early work of the L.M.S.

So one organization led on to another.

v

In not a few cases the same men were office-bearers of more than one of the societies listed above. William Wilberforce and Henry Thornton were remarkable in this respect, as we shall see, but so also were a number of others. Joseph Hardcastle, the City merchant who became the first treasurer of the L.M.S., had already taken an interest in the stopping of the slave trade and in the founding of the Sierra Leone Company. Clarkson wrote much of his *History of the Abolition of the Slave Trade* at Hatcham House where Hardcastle lived. He was also associated with the R.T.S., of which one of his business partners, Joseph Reyner, was treasurer. The early committees both of the L.M.S. and the R.T.S. met at the Hardcastle counting-house in Lower Thames Street, and it was in the same room that in 1804 the Bible Society was formed. The Battersea Baptist minister, Joseph Hughes, became the first secretary of the R.T.S. and then one of the secretaries of the Bible Society, holding both posts till shortly before his death in 1833. One of his first Bible Society colleagues was Josiah Pratt, who in 1802 had become secretary of the C.M.S.

The same names occur again and again in the different subscription lists. Even a purely denominational society like the B.M.S. received the support of many belonging to other branches of the Church. One of the earliest printed subscription lists of the B.M.S. covers the year from October 1797 to October 1798. It records gifts of £10 10s. from Messrs Hardcastle, Reyner and Corsbie (the firm to which Joseph Hardcastle belonged), £5 5s. each from Henry and Robert Thornton and £3 3s. from Samuel Thornton (the three distinguished Anglican evangelicals, two of whom were Members of Parliament), and £1 1s. from the Reverend Basil Woodd, the Anglican evangelical incumbent of Bentinck Chapel, Marylebone; while among the special donations for the Bible translation work which Carey was then beginning there is a further substantial gift from Messrs Hardcastle, Reyner and Corsbie. The B.M.S. subscription list for the following twelve months contains the names of Charles Grant (back from Bengal, and a director of the East India Company and member of the Clapham group), several of the Gurneys (who were Quakers), Hardcastle and Reyner once more, the three Thornton brothers, William Wilberforce, and again Basil Woodd. In return, when the first C.M.S. deputation visited Kettering, Andrew Fuller held one of the plates at the door and solicited contributions.[1]

This generous mutual aid was but the outward expression of a strong common purpose and a deep sense of unity. A. D. Martin, in his biography of the great Dutch missionary Vanderkemp, who became a pioneer of the L.M.S. in South Africa, says: " The Churches were never closer to one another than in those glad and fervent days of missionary beginnings. Episcopalian, Presbyterian, Congregationalist worshipped not so much according to denominational distinctions as according to the fundamental unity of Christ's saving evangel."[2] This is too sweeping a claim. There was at the time much tension between the Church of England and the Nonconformist bodies—the latter still suffered from certain civil disabilities; and there were differences between various parties within the Churches. It was not a period of general amity

---

[1] Stock, *History of the C.M.S.*, i. p. 135.    [2] Op. cit., p. 56.

and co-operation. But the group of men whom we are considering, the founders of the missionary societies, were truly " of one heart and mind," and this is one of their most memorable characteristics.

Josiah Pratt, of the C.M.S., established and edited *The Missionary Register*, which from 1813 to 1855 was a most useful magazine, chronicling the work of all the societies. The most striking evidence of unity and common purpose was probably, however, the organization and support of the Bible Society. This body had from its inception three secretaries, an Anglican, a Nonconformist and a Lutheran. One of the earliest local auxiliaries was that formed at Norwich in 1811. Afterwards there was a party at Earlham Hall, near by, the home of John Gurney, the Quaker. " We had," wrote his son, " a vast party at Earlham, and a remarkable day, a perfectly harmonious mixture of High Church, Low Church, Lutheran, Baptist, Quaker! It was a time which seemed to pull down all barriers of distinction, and to melt us all into a common Christianity." Afterwards, Elizabeth Fry, who was one of John Gurney's eleven children, led the company in prayer. " Now of a truth," said Joseph Hughes, who was one of those present, " I perceive that God is no respecter of persons, but that in every age and nation those who fear Him and work righteousness are accepted by Him." And when later he came to record the occasion he wrote: " We seemed generally to feel like the disciples whose hearts burned within them as they walked to Emmaus."[1] It was because this unity was rare and

[1] See Canton, i. p. 73 f. The quotations are from Hare, *The Gurneys of Earlham*. Borrow's *Lavengro* contains a description of John Gurney. At the second meeting of the Norwich Bible Society, in 1812, young Thomas Fowell Buxton was persuaded to speak. Four years earlier he had married Hannah Gurney, the fifth daughter of the Earlham

newly discovered that it so moved those who shared in it.

Enough has already been said to show how prominent a part in all these movements was taken by laymen. Joseph Timms, the wool stapler, was the only one present at the Kettering meeting in 1792 who was not a minister, but the B.M.S. quickly associated business men in the Midlands and in London with its enterprise. The first board of directors of the L.M.S. consisted of twenty ministers and fourteen laymen. The first committee of the C.M.S. had eleven laymen out of a membership of twenty-four, one a sculptor, one a solicitor, one an upholsterer, one a skinner, one a banker, one a surgeon, one a tea broker, one a silk merchant, and three described in general terms as merchants. Through the action of Josiah Pratt, the far-sighted young secretary of the C.M.S., all thirty-six of the elected members of the Bible Society committee were laymen, fifteen of them members of the Church of England, fifteen from other Christian communions, and six of them foreigners resident in London. The organization of the Wesleyan Methodist Missionary Society was very largely due to the initiative of a group of Leeds laymen, among whom William Dawson was outstanding—" the greatest lay preacher ever given by God to Methodism."[1]

The youth of many of those who took the lead in those exciting times is significant. Carey was thirty-one years old when the B.M.S. was formed, and when household, and had begun to attend the Wheeler Street Chapel, Spitalfields, at which Josiah Pratt preached. " Whatever I have done in my life for Africa, the seeds of it were sown in my heart in Wheeler Street Chapel," was Buxton's verdict thirty years later. Entering Parliament in 1818, Buxton became the close friend of Wilberforce, and was nominated by him as leader in the struggle for slave emancipation. See *Memoirs of Sir Thomas Fowell Buxton* (Everyman edition), p. 24.

[1] Findlay, i. p. 51.

William Ward reached him in India after his seven gruelling years as an indigo planter, the newcomer put down in his diary: " He is very little changed from what I recollected . . . and, blessed be God, a young man still." The leaders in the formation of the L.M.S. were in their early forties. Joseph Hughes was only thirty when he became secretary of the R.T.S., and thirty-four when he added to that office his work for the Bible Society. Josiah Pratt, possessing " rare tact and business capacity "[1] and a wide range of interests, was thirty-four when he was appointed secretary of the C.M.S. There were older men behind them, but executive responsibility in these new ventures was wisely placed on young shoulders, and the results justified the faith that was shown.

VI

Inspiring, feeding and directing this awakened philanthropic and missionary enthusiasm stood the Clapham Sect and those associated with them—the " Saints," as they were scoffingly called, with William Wilberforce their chief glory.[2] It is impossible to exaggerate their influence on the religious and social life of their time, and the debt which modern England owes to them. Yet, apart from Wilberforce, they were none of them popular figures. They had many sneers to endure, besides the biting phrases of Sydney Smith, and the indifference, if not hostility, of many on the episcopal bench. The group has often been described. Thackeray painted a satirical picture in the early pages of *The Newcomes* (1853-5), but the best account is still

[1] *Dictionary of National Biography*, xvi. p. 293.
[2] See J. A. Patten, *These Remarkable Men*, 1945, and E. M. Howse, *Saints in Politics*, 1953.

in Sir James Stephen's famous *Essays in Ecclesiastical Biography* (1849), which was written out of intimate personal knowledge of the whole circle.

In 1792, as already noted, Henry Thornton, M.P. for Southwark, bought a house at the west end of Clapham Common. He was then a young man of thirty-two, of great wealth and singular disinterestedness. His family and that of Wilberforce were connected by marriage, and from 1792 to 1797 the rising young statesman lived with his friend. The famous oval library of the Clapham house had been designed by William Pitt the Elder, and it soon became the meeting-place of a brilliant coterie determined to serve their generation with all the means at their disposal. When Wilberforce married in 1797, he moved no farther than the bounds of Thornton's estate. In a neighbouring house there came to live Charles Grant, recently back from Bengal, and after 1802 a Member of Parliament, like Wilberforce and Henry and Robert Thornton. Nearby were living Lord Teignmouth (formerly Governor-General of India), Granville Sharp, who had refused to take orders in the Church of England that he might more whole-heartedly devote himself to the struggle against slavery, and who added to that task the championship of many other good causes, Zachary Macaulay, the devoted friend of Africa and father of a yet more famous son, and James Stephen, a lawyer of West Indian experience, who had married Wilberforce's sister. All were deeply religious men, owing much to the aged John Newton and the earliest generation of evangelicals. At Clapham Parish Church, where they regularly worshipped, John Venn was rector, and they were also bound to him by close ties of personal friendship.

In and out of Thornton's house came men and women from all parts of the country, of many different walks of life and of a variety of religious persuasions, though it was those who shared the general evangelical attitude to personal religion who felt most quickly at home there. The closest collaborators in the religious interests of the " Saints " were Charles Simeon and Isaac Milner, of Cambridge, and, in London, Richard Cecil, the scholarly and cultured clergyman of St John's, Bedford Row, to whom Josiah Pratt was curate for a time, Thomas Scott, the famous Bible commentator, then at the Lock Chapel, and Basil Woodd of Marylebone. The gifted Hannah More was reckoned of the circle, and both Thornton and Wilberforce made her very substantial gifts for her Sunday Schools in Cheddar and neighbourhood. That Nonconformists were admitted to their homes on terms of intimate familiarity was often charged against the Clapham group by the more snobbish and intolerant of their contemporaries. Thomas Charles, of Bala, who threw in his lot with the Calvinistic Methodists and became the leader in a notable revival of religion in North Wales, was well acquainted with John Newton, a correspondent of Scott's, a prime mover in the starting of the Bible Society, and a frequent visitor at Clapham. Joseph Hughes was Baptist minister at neighbouring Battersea. A score of times during the struggles over the East India Charter, Andrew Fuller, of Kettering, the B.M.S. secretary, might have been found having breakfast with Wilberforce.

The Clapham Sect, with their substantial business interests and growing political responsibilities—particularly those connected with the struggle against the slave trade—interested themselves keenly and sacrificially in the various societies which came into being during the troubled years of the Napoleonic wars. Indeed, many of them were among the founders, and but for them these organizations could never have been launched. We have already noted that a number of gifts were made to the B.M.S. in its early years. Newton, Wilberforce, Thornton, Venn, Cecil, Scott, Woodd and Pratt were all members of the first committee of the C.M.S., and Zachary Macaulay and Charles Simeon joined it shortly afterwards. Wilberforce, Thornton, Granville Sharp, Macaulay, Stephen and Grant were on the first committee of the Bible Society, and Lord Teignmouth became President. Almost all of them were on the committee of the African Institution, which took the place of the Sierra Leone Company. When the Religious Tract Society was formed, partly to circulate Hannah More's tracts, it benefited greatly from their generous help and advice.[1] The Society for the Suppression of Vice was one of Wilberforce's special concerns. As a young man of twenty-five, Henry Thornton had aided William Fox, a Baptist draper, in starting a Society for the Establishment of Sunday Schools, and out of this came the Sunday School Union. Any and every cause of this kind could count on support from Clapham.

Thornton is said to have given away no less than six-sevenths of his income up to the time of his marriage and at least one-third of it after that. This was princely munificence, and it was joined to a shrewd judgment on which Wilberforce much relied. It was the latter who was the brilliant centre of the Sect. Professor Coupland

---

[1] Macaulay, Hardcastle, Shrubsole and Rowland Hill were on the committee of the R.T.S. in London, while Fuller, Bogue, Burder and Thomas Charles were among the " country members."

thus describes him: " Small, slender, frail, so short-sighted that the peering posture of his body was likened as time went on to the letter S, with a whimsical face which would almost have been ugly but for the brilliant deep-set eyes; sensitive but not shy, never still and rarely silent, he possessed all the gifts—the oddity and charm, the unselfconsciousness, the flow of witty conversation, the drawing-room accomplishments of mimicry and song, the whole-hearted love of amuse-ment—which the fashionable world required of its favourites."[1] In the year of his marriage he set out his religious faith in *A Practical View of Christianity*,[2] a book which quickly secured immense influence in evangelical circles, and which he most impressively illustrated by his life. On the day Wilberforce died, Fowell Buxton, speaking in the House of Commons, applied to him Cowper's lines:

> A veteran warrior in the Christian field,
> Who never saw the sword he could not wield.

He and his friends were not only the benefactors of the slaves; they played an essential part in laying the foundations of the world-wide Christian Church of our own time.

## VII

It is difficult to imagine a greater contrast than that between the little company of Baptist ministers who met in Kettering, and one of the gatherings of friends in Henry Thornton's library at Clapham. Yet they were contemporaries and had a common concern for the

---

[1] *The British Anti-Slavery Movement*, p. 71.

[2] Its full title was *A Practical View of the Prevailing Religious System of Professed Christians in the Higher and Middle Classes in this Country contrasted with Real Christianity*.

fulfilment of their Christian obligations, and there were personal links between them. To complete these glimpses of the men who started the great missionary societies we turn to a third group, different from either of these others yet connected with them both.

In the student world the new missionary vision was first seen by a company of young Americans. In 1806, a group of students of Williams College, in Massachusetts, caught by a thunderstorm on their way to a prayer meeting, sheltered under a haystack, and after conversation and prayer about the moral darkness of Asia, decided to consecrate their lives to missionary service. A stone column now marks the spot which is regarded as " The Birthplace of American Foreign Missions."[1] There were no societies then in America, but when one of his friends pointed this out and suggested that the young men had been somewhat premature, Mills, the leader of the band, replied: " We can do it if we will." He and three others of the haystack party moved shortly afterwards to Andover Theological Institution, where they made the acquaintance of Adoniram Judson and Samuel Nott. The establishment of the American Board of Commissioners for Foreign Missions was the direct result of their combined pleas.

By then the new leaven was also beginning to work on this side of the Atlantic among the undergraduates of Cambridge, thanks to the enthusiasm of Charles Simeon, but we can best see it entering the university world here by noting what happened in Scotland.

In 1796 Simeon went on a journey north of the

[1] Latourette, op. cit., iv. p. 80, says, " The entire story of the haystack meeting is somewhat uncertain. The year is in doubt and the details are debatable."

border and preached at Moulin. He thought it a "barren and dry sermon," and perhaps not many could understand his southern accent, but the kirk minister was kindled by its fervour, and from then on his influence on his people had a new quality. That influence contributed in important measure to the early training of Alexander Duff. Scotland showed itself somewhat reluctant to join officially in the missionary movement. When a motion in favour of foreign missions was before the General Assembly in the very year of Simeon's sermon it was strongly opposed. "Moderator, rax me that Bible!" cried old Dr John Erskine,[1] of Greyfriars, the friend of Whitefield and Jonathan Edwards, and an eager supporter of the new enterprises. In spite of his appeal to Scripture, however, the motion was defeated, and such help as was given by Scotland came in gifts to the English societies. Considerable amounts were gathered for the B.M.S. by Andrew Fuller, who was indefatigable in his journeyings. Generous support came also to the L.M.S., and it was under its auspices that Robert Haldane, as will later be told, sought unsuccessfully to start a mission in Bengal. In 1821 the Glasgow Missionary Society began a mission in Kaffraria and two years later the Scottish Missionary Society began work in India. It was not until 1824, however, that a committee was set up which committed the Scottish Church as a whole to the missionary cause. An outstanding part in this decision was taken by Thomas Chalmers, then in the midst of his very influential career as preacher and

---

[1] It was Erskine who had in 1784 drawn the attention of the Northamptonshire Baptist ministers to the writings of Jonathan Edwards, and particularly to his work on prayer. A description of Erskine's preaching will be found in Scott's *Guy Mannering*, ch. xxxvii. The authenticity of the incident about the Bible has been challenged.

teacher. He had just completed his first exciting session as Professor of Moral Philosophy at St Andrews University, and there young Duff was among his students.

Chalmers had had a brilliant academic career, and had been licensed to preach in 1799, when only nineteen years old, but his religion was then of a rather perfunctory kind. His chief interest was in chemistry and the new physical sciences. He had shared in the excitement at Napoleon's threatened invasion, and had joined the volunteers. He had written a pamphlet on political economy shortly after the issue of Napoleon's " Berlin Decrees." Then came serious illness and a profound spiritual change. He was deeply stirred by Wilberforce's *Practical View* and also by the accounts of the early work of the B.M.S. In the agitation over the East India Charter, and in the subsequent missionary controversies, Chalmers showed himself a staunch champion of Carey and his friends. The able young Scotsman was soon recognized as one of the chief Scottish " evangelicals," and a most gifted exponent of the power of the Gospel and of its universal application.[1] During his first session at St Andrews the students' enthusiasm was kindled not only by his eloquent and forceful lecturing, but by his regular Sunday School activity, and by his missionary concern. The St Andrews University Missionary Society was formed, an organization foreshadowing very closely the beginnings two generations later of the Student Volunteer Missionary Union. His son-in-law claims that " the most extraordinary spiritual product " of

[1] Wilberforce and Canning once climbed in at the window of a crowded South London chapel to hear him preach, Canning later using a part of the sermon in one of his parliamentary speeches. See *Memoirs of Sir T. F. Buxton*, p. 183.

the five years Chalmers spent as professor at St Andrews was " the number of those who out of that small band devoted themselves to missionary labour."[1]

Thanks to Chalmers and others, when at length the General Assembly officially adopted a scheme of missionary policy it fixed upon India as its field, and committed itself definitely to work of an educational character. Slowly there shaped itself in Duff's mind the conviction that he ought to offer himself for this service. Thomas Chalmers was throughout his friend and counsellor. Robert Morrison, home after his first spell in China, visited Chalmers at St Andrews in 1825; two years later, Joshua Marshman, of Serampore, stayed with him. The Professor's enthusiasm for the missionary cause mounted as it became better informed, and he took the keenest interest in the gradual turning of Duff's mind towards work abroad. On August 12th, 1829, it was he who presided over the ordination of Duff as the first official missionary of the Church of Scotland.

[1] Hanna, *Memoirs of Dr Chalmers*, iii. p. 202.

# CHAPTER IV

# THE MOTIVE AND THE MESSAGE

" The whole trend of development, one discovers
with awe, seems to confront the missionary movement
with its original motive, that is, the certitude of
having the apostolic obligation towards the world
of witnessing to Christ and His new Kingdom."
H. Kraemer, *The Christian Message in a Non-Christian
World*. E.H.P., 1938, p. 59.

I

WHAT WAS THE MOTIVE behind the outburst of missionary
zeal which showed itself so powerfully during the years
when Napoleon dominated Europe? What was the
faith of the men who formed the great missionary
societies and were responsible for so much other
philanthropic activity? What were their outlook and
hope?

There are many strange illusions and misconceptions
about their beliefs. They are often thought of as
ignorant, narrow, bigoted and pietistic, moved by
unattractive and unworthy motives, and dominated by
the fear of hell. Even those who honour their enthusiasm
and achievement have been ready to credit the most
strange parodies of their beliefs. For this the novelists
must be held responsible to a considerable extent. The
exuberant genius of Dickens made Mrs Jellyby and
Chadband for ever memorable, and Thackeray drew
his picture of Sophia Alethea Hobson (Mrs Thomas
Newcome), " the bishopess of Clapham." But these are

caricatures, not historical portraits, and they were written—and this is of great importance and significance —in the middle of the nineteenth century, when, it may be confessed, there had been some descent from the first heights of vision and conviction. Two generations had passed since Carey and Melvill Horne, Coke and Haweis, Simeon and Wilberforce, had roused Christian people to their missionary obligations. The lives and writings of these men are a safer guide to their temper and outlook than the pages, brilliant and entertaining as they are, of Dickens and Thackeray; and we are, perhaps, today better able to understand the generation that faced Napoleon than were the mid-Victorians.

The pioneers wrote and spoke as men emancipated from intellectual and theological fetters, as men of wide and generous sympathies, as men in touch with all the great questions of their day. They were deeply stirred by events in Europe and by the widespread indifference to the Christian faith and the Christian ethic which was evident in this country. They were men who had found in their personal religion the secret of confidence and power in a distracted world. Almost all of them had come more or less directly under the influence of what we call the Evangelical Revival, that is, that movement of the Spirit of God which, expressing itself in a variety of ways, gave a new vitality in the second half of the eighteenth century to personal faith, rescuing men not only from gross sins but from an arid intellectualism and a dead formality. The Wesleys and Whitefield were the outstanding agents of the revival, but, as already hinted, it was a wider movement than that usually associated with their names. The general outlook and temper which it produced can be seen at its best in Wilberforce's *Practical View*, and as this came out of the midst of the main group described in the last chapter and was welcomed enthusiastically by almost all of them—Churchmen and Dissenters—it is worthy of some attention.

Wilberforce was thirty-eight years old when he wrote his book, and its appearance in 1797 was compared at the time to an electric shock. The personality of the author, the position he occupied in the councils of the nation, and the style and contents of the book itself combined to excite attention and controversy. Three or four large editions were exhausted within a few months of its appearance, and edition after edition was brought out in the succeeding years, as well as translations into several European languages. Its influence was very widespread, particularly among the " higher and middle classes," to whom Wilberforce specially addressed himself, and among the younger clergy and ministers.[1] Daniel Wilson (later Bishop of Calcutta), in his preface to the fifteenth edition (1826), calls attention to the background against which it was written—" the storm of the French Revolution still raging—an open renunciation of Christianity just made in a great nation—Europe rent asunder with a war, which, after a duration of four or five years, seemed farther than ever from a close—the Church feeble, and full of apprehension—the ministers of state, and the legislature, overwhelmed with schemes of defence abroad and regulation at home—the minds of thoughtful men portending calamities—untold difficulties

[1] Livingstone, in *Journeys and Researches in South Africa*, 1857, p. 4, records that his father's " last application of the rod was on my refusal to peruse Wilberforce's *Practical Christianity*." But at that time the book must have been more than twenty-five years old, for Livingstone was not born till 1813, and it was scientific works and books of travel that were his delight. James Martineau (1805-1900) records the deep influence Wilberforce's book had upon him while he was a schoolboy.

thickening around."[1] At this juncture a man of the character and ability of Wilberforce, a layman, not a cleric, poured out in this book—which was dictated under great pressure of spirit between two sessions of Parliament—his conviction that the only hope for his nation and for the whole world lay in a rediscovery of the essential truths of the Christian Gospel.

There is a strangely familiar ring about much of what he says. He speaks of the formal adherence to Christianity which was conventional, but which really meant very little. Men have their own moral standards, it is true, but they can hardly be called those of Jesus. " The Bible lies on the shelf unopened: and they would be wholly ignorant of its contents, except for what they hear occasionally at church, or for the faint traces which their memories may still retain of the lessons of their earliest infancy." The real state of things can best be judged, suggests Wilberforce, by reading contemporary novels, and seeing how small is the part played in them by the Christian religion. Turning to his own exposition of the faith, he begins boldly by asserting what he knows to be unpopular—that human nature is corrupt, and that the evil in the world, as obvious and blatant then as now, comes from the wickedness of the human heart and the power of " the Prince of this world ". The Christian Gospel is offered to men in their perplexity and distress as light from darkness, release from prison, life from death; and it gives these things to those who put their faith in Jesus Christ, and who in consequence receive His Holy Spirit.

Wilberforce was well aware of all the objections that might be urged—that religious emotion has often been joined to hypocrisy; that what has sometimes been

[1] Op. cit., p. 34.

claimed as religious experience is the result of " the flights of a lively imagination, or the working of a heated brain; in particular, that this love of our Saviour, which has been so warmly recommended, is no better than a vain fervour, which dwells only in the disordered mind of the enthusiast "; that with regard to the Holy Spirit there seems no sure criterion by which to judge men's claims to His guidance. Wilberforce is quite frank. All these things may be admitted, but it yet remains true, he says, that the testimony of the Bible (and of the liturgy of the Church of England, whatever may be said in sermons), reinforced by Christian experience, is that the only source of personal peace and power is in Christ.

Those who discover this endeavour " cordially and unreservedly " to devote themselves to the service of God and the overthrow of the forces of evil; " their bodily and mental faculties, their natural and acquired endowments, their substance, their authority, their time, their influence—all these they consider as belonging to them, not for their own gratification, but as so many instruments to be consecrated to the honour of God, and employed in His service."

This was the faith and this the aim of the members of the Clapham Sect and those allied with them. They felt themselves called to lives of strenuous and constant service in opposition to the manifest evils of their time, because God had spoken a word of redemption to them and to all men in Christ. The moral laxity, the cruel inhumanity, the widespread infidelity and ignorance they felt as a challenge to their most earnest endeavours. They were crusaders for a new and better order, and, though their hopes were not all fulfilled and some of their schemes went sadly wrong, the most reluctant secular historian is compelled to recognize their remarkable achievements and their disinterested spirit. They were realists and they were faced with many unpleasant facts. Towards the end of the *Practical View* Wilberforce confesses that as he looks at the national situation he feels: " We bear upon us but too plainly the marks of a declining empire." But he goes on to a bold and impressive avowal of his " firm persuasion that to the decline of Religion and Morality our national difficulties must both directly and indirectly be chiefly ascribed.

" My only solid hopes for the well-being of my country depend," he continues, " not so much on her fleets and armies, not so much on the wisdom of her rulers, or the spirit of her people, as on the persuasion, that she still contains many who love and obey the Gospel of Christ; that their intercessions may yet prevail; that for the sake of these, heaven may still look upon us with an eye of favour."

There is nothing in Wilberforce's book about foreign missions, save a high tribute to the Moravians, but the outlook and temper portrayed in its pages led Wilberforce and his friends to interest themselves in this cause, as in so many others. Less than two years after the publication of *A Practical View*, Wilberforce joined in the formation of the C.M.S. Men and women in distant lands, whose condition provided abundant evidence of the blindness and sinfulness of human nature, were without any knowledge of Christ. It was the duty and privilege, then, of true Christians to take the Gospel to them. The evangelicals were chiefly moved, not by fear of hell—for themselves or for the heathen—but by gratitude to God, attachment to Christ, and love of their fellows.

II

Instead of Wilberforce's *Practical View* we might take Wesley's hymn book to illustrate the evangelical out-look, for in the preface which he wrote for it in 1780 the Methodist leader claimed it as " a body of practical and experimental divinity," which the poorest and most unlettered of his people would gradually learn by heart. It is full of the characteristic themes of universal redemption and thoroughgoing consecration or, as it was then called, complete sanctification. It opens with the triumphant hymn of Charles Wesley, *O for a thousand tongues to sing my great Redeemer's praise.* This had been written as early as 1739 in the first ardour of his discovery of the secret of personal religion, and it has in it the lines:

> My gracious Master and my God,
>   Assist me to proclaim,
> To spread through all the earth abroad
>   The honour of Thy Name. . . .
>
> Look unto Him, ye nations; own
>   Your God, ye fallen race;
> Look, and be saved through faith alone,
>   Be justified by grace.

John Wesley himself had taken the world as his parish, and Dr Findlay can well claim that " in point of doctrine, the Wesleyan Revival was a reaction against narrowing conceptions of the Gospel and the Church of Christ, whether Calvinistic, sacerdotal, nationalist, or particularist of whatever kind." Characteristic phrases like " general grace," " undistinguishing regard," " universal love," applied frequently in the hymns to the attitude of God towards man, had at first, he points out, a theological rather than a geographical or interracial meaning, "but such language took another aspect in the crisis of that age, when through world-commerce and the clash of arms the sinners were confronted with men of foreign climes and colours."[1] Among Charles Wesley's hymns is one "For the Mahometans" and one "For the Heathen."

As we have seen, it was Thomas Coke, the Methodist, who as early as 1784 projected a "Society for the Establishment of Missions among the Heathens." Had his scheme been taken up, it would have been the earliest of the societies with a specifically missionary purpose. It is significant that Coke addressed his appeal "To All the Real Lovers of Mankind," and stated his confidence that many men of "good Sense, Integrity, great Piety, and amazing Zeal" would be ready to volunteer as missionaries, their aim being to "promote the Kingdom of Christ, and the present and eternal welfare of their Fellow Creatures." Here is no narrow creed, no morbid outlook.

Two historic missionary pamphlets claim attention in this connection, namely Carey's *Enquiry into the Obligation of Christians to use means for the Conversion of the Heathens*, published in 1792, and Melvill Horne's *Letters on Missions; addressed to the Protestant Ministers of the British Churches*, which appeared in 1794. Both were of considerable importance for the beginnings of the modern missionary movement and the founding of the great societies.

[1] Findlay, i. p. 31. It is surprising to find that this aspect is not dealt with in J. E. Rattenbury's otherwise thorough and acute study, *The Evangelical Doctrines of Charles Wesley's Hymns*, 1941. But note p. 79: " It has been generally held that the Methodist Revival was based on the fear of hell, but in point of fact, though the wrath of God was always in the background, the Wesleys themselves appealed very little to this fear and warned their preachers against doing so."

Carey's eighty-seven pages represented the fruit of his thought and prayer during five or six years. It surprises the modern reader by its directness and simplicity. There is no pietistic or sentimental appeal, no theological arguing, but a plain statement of his case, backed by an impressive array of facts. Dr George Smith, writing in 1885, called it the " first and still greatest missionary treatise in the English language,"[1] and as a brief but cogent setting forth of the gist of the matter it is still supreme. A short introduction urges that those who use the Lord's Prayer ought to inform themselves as to the religious state of the world, and the pamphlet is then divided into five sections. The first is " an Enquiry whether the Commission given by our Lord to His disciples be not still binding on us." This is clearly directed to the attitude of the Reformers, to which allusion has already been made, and which was still accepted in many quarters. Was the command to teach all nations intended only for the Apostles? If not, then only the impossibility of fulfilling it would exempt us from doing our part. That it is not impossible is shown by what has been done by Jesuits and Moravians, and also by English traders. Nor are we exempt because many in this land are " as ignorant as the South-Sea savages."

The second section of the *Enquiry* consists of " a short Review of former Undertakings for the Conversion of the Heathen " beginning with Pentecost and giving in a dozen pages an outline of the progress recorded in *Acts*, then a few references to the expansion of the Church in the early centuries and in the Middle Ages, and on to the sporadic seventeenth- and eighteenth-century efforts among the Indians of America and those

[1] *The Life of William Carey* (Everyman edition), p. 28.

of India and the East Indies. A " Survey of the present State of the World " forms the third section, and its tables must have involved long hours of research. The countries of the world are set out continent by continent, their length and breadth are given, the number of their inhabitants and the religions to be found in each of them. The fourth section urges " the Practicability of something being done, more than what is done, for the Conversion of the Heathen," replying specifically to certain common excuses. Then in the last section the immediate practical steps that might be taken are clearly indicated: first, fervent and united prayer, next the energetic use of the new opportunities provided by the opening up of the world to trade, and finally, the organization of a society with a committee charged to send out missionaries. Carey appeals to Christians of all denominations, but drives home his challenge most pointedly to his own Baptist friends. " Surely," he concludes, " it is worth while to lay ourselves out with all our might, in promoting the cause and kingdom of Christ."[1]

Together with Carey's famous sermon, this little pamphlet had a decisive part in the formation of the Baptist Missionary Society, and also attracted attention outside the Baptist ranks, though there is no evidence that it had a very wide circulation. It was warmly praised by Melvill Horne, and it was also commended in the early appeals of the London Missionary Society.

Melvill Horne had succeeded the saintly Fletcher in the living of Madeley, and later had a brief spell in the famous Olney curacy, in which both John Newton and

[1] In the preceding paragraphs I have adapted certain passages from an article of mine on the *Enquiry* in *The International Review of Missions,* April 1942.

Thomas Scott had preceded him. In 1791 the Sierra Leone Company received its charter from Parliament. It was to be a settlement for freed slaves, and Professor Coupland describes it as a " unique experiment in philanthropic colonization."[1] Granville Sharp was President of the Company, Henry Thornton was Chairman, and Wilberforce, Grant and Hardcastle were among the directors. The first governor was John Clarkson—brother of Thomas Clarkson—and this arduous position was occupied from 1794 to 1799 by Zachary Macaulay. The Company had many vicissitudes, but in 1807 Sierra Leone was taken over as a Crown Colony. There is little doubt that it was their close association in the chequered affairs of the Company which paved the way for the later co-operation of this group of evangelical Anglicans and Dissenters in many another humanitarian and missionary enterprise. Melvill Horne spent fourteen months as Anglican chaplain in Sierra Leone. He had hoped to do some missionary work in the interior, in addition to his official duties, but returned to England, because, as he puts it in the singularly candid and ingenuous preface to his *Letters*, " I could not persuade myself to take a sickly, delicate woman and young children, and place them in an African wood, where I must leave them for one half of my time, while I was engaged in rambling from village to village." The nine letters were written while he was at Sierra Leone, but published after his return; they form, with the preface, a pamphlet of 156 pages. There is much repetition in them, but they are a very frank and passionate plea for missionary activity on the part of the Church, and are of considerable historical interest.

[1] *The British Anti-Slavery Movement*, p. 84.

Horne attacks the sectarian controversies of his day, which seem to him foolish and wicked in the face of the tremendous happenings in France and the state of the heathen world. Again there is something strangely contemporary in what is said. Equally shocking to Horne is the indifference of so many avowedly Christian people. " Provided we may live in peace and comfort, do a little good in England, accumulate fortunes, marry wives, take care of our children, and *creep* into heaven at last, we appear satisfied to leave our Master to propagate His own Gospel in the world."[1] He pleads for a flaming evangelism to remove the reproach that " Greenland is, perhaps, the only Heathen Country, in which the genuine religion of Christ has gained a *firm* footing for several centuries."[2] All the efforts since the Reformation, heroic as some of them have been, have yielded perhaps one hundred thousand genuine converts to Christianity.

Much more boldness is wanted, says Horne. Missionaries should be sent out in companies of ten or twelve, preferably unmarried, and with some trade or occupation by which they can support themselves. Each one must remember, however, that he is " a preacher of the Gospel, and that it is not so much moral truths as Gospel principles and motives that he is to instil into his auditors."[3] These principles centre for Horne on the Incarnation and death of the Son of God for the redemption of sinful man.

Horne's fifth and sixth letters deal at length with the qualifications needed by missionaries, and how individuals may satisfy themselves as to their call to this work. They contain a number of shrewd remarks, of which this may serve as an example: " Too often we

[1] Op. cit., p. 13.     [2] Op. cit., p. 26.     [3] Op. cit., p. 47.

deceive ourselves by supposing constitutional vivacity is Christian zeal." In the seventh letter he deals with some of the current objections to missions, including that interpretation of prophecy which anticipates first " the destruction of the Roman Anti-Christ, then the conversion of the Jews, and last of all, the fullness of the Gentiles; in which work the converted Jews, it is thought, will be the principal instruments."[1] He deals too with the attitude to heathen religion which would leave it alone, trusting in the generous judgment of God upon it, and also with the charge that missions are dangerous politically. The two final letters are a fervent appeal for a Christian discipleship as ardent as that shown by men in the service of their country and of their own fortunes. " Our meeting with so little persecution for righteousness' sake is one demonstration that our religion does not over much gall the Devil and his children."[2]

So much for Horne's *Letters*, which reached circles far wider than those touched by Carey's *Enquiry*.[3] Both these men, the one in India, the other in England, lived on to see undreamed-of developments in the missionary activity of the Church, for which they had so earnestly pleaded.

---

[1] Op. cit., p. 99.          [2] Op. cit., p. 129.

[3] Horne sent a copy of his *Letters* to Carey in India, and in the B.M.S. *Periodical Accounts*, i. pp. 231 f., there is printed a letter of thanks to the author. " My soul is certainly akin to yours," writes Carey. In the *Baptist Register*, ii. pp. 249-55, will be found " A Sermon by the Rev. Mr Melvill Horne, late one of the chaplains of the Sierra Leone Co. The *only* discourse which has been delivered to the Natives in the western parts of Africa. Preached about 1793." Horne became a director of the L.M.S.

III

The attack upon sectarianism which occurs more than once in Horne's pages met with an eager response among the founders of " The Missionary Society," now known as the L.M.S.

" The missionary," said Horne, " must be far removed from narrow bigotry, and possess a spirit truly catholic. It is not Calvinism, it is not Arminianism, but Christianity, that he is to teach. It is not the hierarchy of the Church of England; it is not the principles of Protestant Dissenters, that he has in view to propagate. His object is to serve the Church Universal."[1]

Congregationalists, Presbyterians and Anglicans joined in the founding of the L.M.S. No formal subscription to any statement of faith or ecclesiastical order was required of the missionaries, though it is claimed that " almost every early missionary would have had no difficulty whatever in signing the full Westminster Confession."[2] On May 9th, 1796, the Directors adopted a notable declaration, which remains a guiding principle of the Society, though its main support comes now from the Congregational Churches of Britain.

" As the union of God's people of various Denominations, in carrying on this great Work, is a most desirable Object, so, to prevent, if possible, any cause of future dissension, it is declared to be a fundamental principle of the Missionary Society, that our design is not to send Presbyterianism, Independency, Episcopacy, or any other form of Church Order and Government (about which there may be differences

[1] Op. cit., p. 60.    [2] Lovett, i. p. 48.

of opinion among serious Persons), but the Glorious Gospel of the blessed God to the Heathen: and that it shall be left (as it ever ought to be left) to the minds of the Persons whom God may call into the fellowship of His Son from among them to assume for themselves such form of Church Government, as to them shall appear most agreeable to the Word of God."[1]

The public declarations and appeals made at the founding of the L.M.S. differed little from the statements already quoted. David Bogue, who was by birth and training a Scotsman, had rather more to say about the perishing souls of the heathen and the gross darkness of the pagan and Mohammedan world. George Burder, a Congregationalist, placed his emphasis on the opportunities created by the revival of religion, the discoveries of Captain Cook and the happenings in France, terrible as they were. " Is there not a general apprehension that the Lord is about to produce some great event? " he asked. " Already we have witnessed the most astonishing transactions; and is it not probable that the great Disposer of all is now about, by shaking terribly the nations, to establish that spiritual and extensive Kingdom which cannot be shaken? "[2] Thomas Haweis, an Anglican, preaching on the Great Commission, thus defined the message which was to be carried abroad:

" We appeal to the experience of all ages, what ever did, or ever can control the unruly wills and affections of sinful men, but the preaching the Cross of our Lord Jesus Christ: by whom, saith St Paul,

[1] Note Livingstone's testimony to the appeal this made to him some forty years later. See *Journeys and Researches in South Africa*, 1857, p. 5.

[2] Quoted by Lovett, i. p. 21.

*the world is crucified unto me, and I unto the world.*
Without this, what could a missionary effect in a
heathen land? How poor, how unavailing would
be all the weapons of vain philosophy and false
Christianity! *Embelle telum sine ictu.* Brethren, our
whole success will depend upon this one point; if
Christ be preached—only preached, always preached
—then shall we see the power of His death and
resurrection, and the Lord will add again *daily to His
church of such as shall be saved.*"[1]

These statements may be compared with the careful
analysis made by Dr Stock of the first five Annual
Sermons preached for the C.M.S. They were delivered
in the years 1801-5, and the preachers all came from
the circle of the Clapham Sect. All save one, it is
interesting to note, took texts from the New Testament.

" There are features common to all," says Dr Stock.
" In not one of them is the Lord's Last Command
prominent. The leading thought is usually the
wickedness and misery of Heathendom; and the
motive chiefly appealed to is that of pity. . . . Scott
refers, as do most of the early preachers, to the question
of the future state of the Heathen who have not heard
the Gospel—a subject that frequently came up at the
Eclectic meetings. Generally speaking, the preachers
do not dogmatize on the point; but they urge that as
we certainly have no positive knowledge that the
Heathen *are* saved, it is our plain duty to try to save
them."[2]

Canon Storr was no doubt right in saying that the
bedrock of the older evangelicalism was the authority
of the written word, the inspiration of the letter of

[1] Ibid., p. 29.        [2] Stock, i. p. 76.

Scripture.[1] This is fairly clear in Wilberforce's *Practical View*, though it contains nothing remotely like the "fundamentalism" of the late nineteenth century. It is indeed interesting to see how small a part appeal to texts played in the missionary apologetic of the period, and how careful were Carey and Horne, for example, to insist on the obscurity of prophecy and hence the unwisdom of pressing particular interpretations of it.

Granville Sharp, as he grew older, became more and more obsessed with such questions, and once tried to convince the Whig leader, Fox, that the references to the Little Horn in *Daniel* explained the future policy of Napoleon and the Czar of Russia. Joseph Hardcastle, we are told, "was numbered among many good men, who, through the gloom of present disaster, discerned afar off the rising of a brighter sun than had yet beamed upon our ruined world. Over the downfall of popish tyranny and superstition, they saw infidelity rearing its blood-stained crest, and unmasking before the universe its hideous features. But they also beheld altars overthrown, which were stained with the blood of the saints and martyrs of Jesus, and sceptres broken, which had been wielded against the Kingdom of God. They were assured by prophecy, that the reign of Satan was drawing to its close, that the world was not for ever doomed to groan beneath his iron rod; and amidst the earthquake of political convulsions, they waited to hail the morning of the latter-day glory, already spread upon the mountains, and gilding their summits with the promise of millennial blessedness."[2] Daniel Wilson, in his 1826 edition of Wilberforce's book, hints that the

---

[1] *The Development of English Theology in the Nineteenth Century*, p. 73. The whole of Chapter IV is relevant.

[2] John Morrison, *The Fathers and Founders of the L.M.S.*, 1839, i. p. 321.

time has come to prepare for the second coming of Christ. But these are exceptions to the general attitude, and could be paralleled from the records of any generation, not least our own. The characteristic outlook was one of confidence in God's overruling government of the world amid all the tumultuous events of the time, a glad acceptance of salvation through faith in Christ, an eager desire to serve Him, a deep and true concern for ignorant and suffering humanity in every part of the earth, and a glad hope in the speedy dawning of a brighter day.

This may be seen in the hymns which the missionary movement made specially its own. One or two were already there to its hand. As early as 1719 Isaac Watts had prepared his metrical version of the seventy-second *Psalm*:

> Jesus shall reign where'er the sun
> Doth his successive journeys run,

but it did not come into wide use until the early years of the nineteenth century. In 1772 William Williams, a Welsh clergyman who was influenced by the Evangelical Revival, wrote *O'er the gloomy hills of darkness*, which achieved a popularity at missionary meetings second only to that of Edward Perronet's *All hail the power of Jesu's name*, which had first appeared in 1779. The Sheffield editor, James Montgomery, the son of a Moravian missionary, provided the new movement with many of its best-known hymns; but we may close this chapter by quoting one of far less distinction than those just mentioned.[1]

---

[1] Neither has it the intrinsic merit of the two hymns by Charles Wesley that have the same first line.

It was written in 1795, and was the work of William Shrubsole, in many ways a typical figure of the period. Shrubsole was a highly respected layman, who came to occupy an important position in the Bank of England. For the first three years of its history, he was one of the secretaries of the L.M.S. He was also connected with the Religious Tract Society. In 1804, he was appointed one of the first members of the Bible Society committee, ranking as one of the Church of England representatives. But ecclesiastical ties meant little to the warm-hearted Shrubsole, and he was ready to listen to anyone who seemed to possess the root of evangelical religion. His hymn illustrates many of the points we have been making. It is untheological, but the French Revolution and the wars in Europe were clearly in the mind of the writer, as well as the condition of the heathen world and the special position of the Jewish people.

> Arm of the Lord, awake! awake!
> Put on Thy strength, the nations shake;
> And let the world, adoring, see
> Triumphs of mercy wrought by Thee!
>
> Say to the heathen, from Thy throne,
> " I am Jehovah, God alone! "
> Thy voice their idols shall confound,
> And cast their altars to the ground.
>
> No more let human blood be spilt,
> Vain sacrifice for human guilt!
> But to each conscience be applied
> The blood that flowed from Jesu's side.
>
> Arm of the Lord, Thy power extend,
> Let Mahomet's imposture end;
> Break superstition's papal chain,
> And the proud scoffer's rage restrain.

Let Zion's time of favour come;
O bring the tribes of Israel home;
And let our wondering eyes behold
Gentiles and Jews in Jesu's fold!

Almighty God, Thy grace proclaim
In every clime, of every name,
Till adverse powers before Thee fall,
And crown the Saviour Lord of all!

# CHAPTER V

# THE SOCIETIES GAIN A FOOTHOLD

" The true makers of history are not to be found on
the surface of events among the successful politicians
or the successful revolutionaries; these are the
servants of events. Their masters are the spiritual
men whom the world knew not, the unregarded
agents of the creative action of the Spirit." Christopher Dawson, *Religion and the Modern State*. Sheed
and Ward, 1935, p. 97.

I

THE ENTHUSIASTS who formed the missionary societies
during the fateful days of the Napoleonic struggle
succeeded gradually in directing the official interest
and energy of their Churches to the work abroad.
This was their great achievement. The forerunners
considered in a previous chapter were very few in
number, and their venturings, significant and memorable as they now appear, were not part of the main
stream of the Christian activity of their day. They were
exceptional, isolated and ill-supported. In the last
years of the eighteenth century and the early decades of
the nineteenth, however, we see the slow stirrings of the
Christian conscience in one body after another, until
it could be claimed that the whole Church was at
length awake to the challenge of the heathen
world.

It meant a revolution in the Christian outlook, and it
did not come in a day. Indeed, those who with such

high hopes and noble purposes established the missionary societies soon discovered that it was easier to set up an organization than it was to find suitable agents, easier to appoint agents than to get them safely overseas, easier to get men and women to the mission fields than to accomplish successful evangelism. The times were uncertain and perilous. There was still much prejudice to overcome, and Britain was at war. Vested interest at home and abroad allied itself with religious conservatism. Again and again, the most carefully laid plans ended in seeming disaster. We belong to a generation that has come to think of missionary work as a natural, rather prosaic and some would say old-maidish line of Christian activity, and have forgotten what a new and exacting enterprise it was one hundred and fifty years ago.

To engage in it demanded a great act of faith, and the promoters had gradually to learn the best methods of procedure. After the baptism of the first Bengali—seven years after Carey's arrival in India—Marshman of Serampore described what had happened in a way which indicates clearly the doubts which must not infrequently have assailed men both here and abroad. " The conversion and transformation of one Hindu," he wrote, " was like a decisive experiment in natural philosophy, of universal application. The divine grace which changed one Indian's heart, could obviously change a hundred thousand."[1] While, to take an illustration of another kind, Thomas Chalmers, the staunch Presbyterian, rejoiced in the establishment of the C.M.S. because he wanted to see as many varieties of method tried as possible. " I like to see the experiments multiplied and diversified in every

[1] Quoted by S. Pearce Carey, *William Carey*, 8th edition, p. 210.

7—GWC

conceivable way," he told the students of St Andrews.[1]
Here we can give only a few isolated glimpses of the
missionary pioneers as they began their service abroad.

II

The first great struggle was for the right even to
enter the British possessions in India, and it was a
struggle that lasted twenty years.

At the instigation of the erratic ship's doctor,
John Thomas, the newly formed B.M.S. was led to
fix on Bengal as the first scene of its operation, Carey
volunteering to return with Thomas to India. That
meant that permits must be secured from the East
India Company. This organization, one half trading,
one half political and administrative, was at the time
firmly set against anything like religious propaganda
or proselytizing within its territories. Its 1698 Charter
provided for a chaplain in every garrison and principal
factory, and enjoined on such chaplains the duty of
learning the native languages, " the better to enable
them to instruct the Gentoos[2] that are servants or
slaves of the same Company in the Protestant religion."
But this was honoured in the breach, not the observance. The company wanted no interference with the
natives, least of all by Dissenters, who often showed
unwelcome Radical sympathies. The revision of the
Charter was under consideration in 1793, within a
few months of the founding of the B.M.S. Influenced
by Charles Grant, but recently home from Bengal,
Wilberforce sought to secure measures for " the

[1] Hanna, *Memoirs of Dr Chalmers*, iii. p. 193.
[2] An Anglo-Indian adaptation of the Portuguese *gentio*, Gentile, used
in the seventeenth century of the pagan inhabitants of Hindoostan to
distinguish them from the Mohammedans.

gradual advancement of the people in useful knowledge and in religious and moral improvement," but his practical suggestions provoked a violent reaction from the Board of Directors in Leadenhall Street, and from others who were becoming increasingly nervous at the developments in revolutionary France. Wilberforce's attempt failed. " Our territories in Hindoostan," he lamented, " twenty millions of people included, are left in the undisturbed and peaceful possession, and committed to the providential protection, of Brama."

The years from 1793 to 1813 were indeed a dark period in the history of Christianity in India. Every possible discouragement was put in the way of missionary effort by the East India Company. It was soon obvious that Carey and Thomas stood no chance of getting the necessary permits. They therefore decided to take the risk of setting out without them. A first abortive start was made with the help of a ship's captain who was personally acquainted with Thomas, but the latter's financial embarrassments caused their return within a few days, and when they set out again it was on a Danish merchantman, and with the whole of Carey's family. The long voyage round the Cape took five months. It seemed best to disembark in a native boat at the mouth of the Hooghly and to try to slip unobserved into Bengal.

Into the struggles of the next six years it is impossible here to enter. Carey had somehow to earn a livelihood to support his sick wife and growing family. He first became a settler in the Sundarban jungle, and then an indigo planter. Often his heart must have failed him. Only a man of the strongest faith and persistence could have endured such disappointments and hardships,

to which were added the disapproving perplexities
of his friends in England, who could not understand
what he was at. The only helper the B.M.S. could
send out to him during those years got into Bengal
by registering as a gentleman's servant. Nevertheless,
Carey held to his missionary purpose, and laid the
foundations of his later amazing linguistic achievements.

The East India Company showed no disposition
to alter its attitude. Robert Haldane, of Airthrey, a
wealthy Scottish layman, inspired by reading the first
number of the *Periodical Accounts of the B.M.S.*, journeyed
down to Gosport in 1796 to see David Bogue, and
proposed to him that they should together go out to
Bengal on a mission financed by Haldane, but under
the auspices of the recently formed L.M.S. They
fixed boldly on Benares as the city where they would
settle, and Haldane made a direct approach for
permission to the President of the Board of Control,
whom he had known from childhood. This was followed
up by all the influence that the Clapham Sect and their
friends could exert, but all to no purpose. The Court
of Directors, they were informed, " have weighty
and substantial reasons which induce them to decline a
compliance with your request."[1] There was perhaps
some suspicion of Haldane's political sympathies, and
some additional prejudice because he was a member of
the Church of Scotland. The main trouble, however,
was that neither Whitehall nor Leadenhall Street
nor Calcutta wanted any kind of missionary work in
the Indian territories. The project had, therefore, to
be abandoned, for a man of Haldane's eminence and

[1] January 1797. See Alexander Haldane, *The Lives of Robert and
James Haldane*, 1853 edition, p. 117. In 1799 the brothers organized the
first Congregational Church in Scotland, and in 1808 both adopted
Baptist views.

position could not steal into India as Carey had done.

Undeterred by what had happened, the B.M.S. in 1799 sent a fresh party of missionaries to Bengal. They found temporary shelter at the little Danish colony of Serampore, and when Carey had completely failed to get permission for them to live and work on British territory, he decided to join them there. Thus it was that the famous mission settlement of Serampore came into existence, Carey finding among the new recruits Marshman and Ward, whose names were destined to be imperishably associated with his. At Serampore, under the Danish flag, where they could not be dislodged or molested by the East India Company, they formed a community on the Moravian pattern, and began extensive translation, printing, educational, philanthropic and evangelistic work.

The next B.M.S. recruit was ready in 1802. Charles Grant strongly advised Andrew Fuller not to raise the question of a missionary permit with the E.I.C. Directors, and the young man and his wife were therefore sent first in an American vessel to New York. The trip across the Atlantic took sixty-one days, and on the way they were involved in a serious collision. After some difficulty, passages were secured on a ship sailing from Philadelphia to Calcutta. This meant another five months' wearisome sailing. The total cost of the outfit and voyage from England to Calcutta of this one couple was £435, but it was decided to send the next party of four recruits by the same route. They all got safely to Serampore, and were soon busily engaged there and in the various sub-stations of the growing mission.

When in 1806, however, two more missionaries arrived in an American ship, the Calcutta authorities took vigorous action against them, and the case seemed likely to threaten the friendly relations between Britain and Denmark. The struggle against Napoleon was at its height. A mutiny of sepoys at Vellore, in July 1806, involving the massacre of a number of British soldiers, contributed to the nervousness of the authorities. A strong anti-missionary spirit was shown both in Bengal and in England. It was then that Sydney Smith uttered his famous gibe about " the nest of consecrated cobblers." To avoid further trouble, Carey sent one of the newcomers with a colleague to establish a mission in Burma, and not for another five years did any new Baptist missionaries leave England. Then, in 1811, two more travelled out to Serampore via America. They had not long arrived before Calcutta officials ordered their immediate return to England, together with that of one of their predecessors, who had used the American route. For some months a very complicated and tense situation existed between Serampore and Calcutta. In the meantime, however, in England, the battle had been won. Castlereagh's India Bill, which incorporated new Charter regulations for the E.I.C., provided for the granting of licences to persons desirous of going to India for the purpose of promoting " the religious and moral improvement " of the native inhabitants.

The struggle in England had been a hard one. The experiences of the Baptist missionaries had been watched with keen sympathy and growing indignation by their fellow-Christians, but the alleviation of the position taxed the combined strength of all the missionary bodies and their supporters. The L.M.S., since the failure of Robert Haldane to get a permit for India, had been awaiting the moment when the Charter would come up for revision. As the time drew nearer, Thomas Coke, the Methodist, became more and more active in stimulating public opinion. The Clapham Sect, led by Wilberforce, Thornton and Grant, marshalled their forces. They had done much to help the Baptist missionaries during the critical years of their early struggles, and, unwilling to challenge the authorities directly, as the B.M.S. had done, had rendered most effective service to the Christian cause in India by securing the appointment, under the E.I.C., of a number of evangelical chaplains.

Such men were badly needed. Sir John Shore (later Lord Teignmouth) reported in 1795, while Governor-General, that the clergy in Bengal " with some exceptions " were " not respectable characters." " A black coat is no security for the general relaxation of morals," he declared. It was Charles Simeon, of Cambridge, who took the lead in this matter. His friend, David Brown, went to Calcutta as chaplain to the Military Orphan Asylum as early as 1787, and during a stay of a quarter of a century rendered outstanding service, interesting himself in a boarding school for Hindus and many other beneficent enterprises. Ten years later, Claudius Buchanan arrived as an E.I.C. chaplain —a remarkable man, who, after a wandering youth, had been led to Christ by John Newton, and who had been educated at Cambridge at the expense of Henry Thornton. Buchanan and Brown were both chosen by Lord Wellesley to help with the Fort William College, at which Carey—as the only man in Bengal who was competent—became Professor of Sanskrit and Bengali. Buchanan gave away much of his salary in prizes to the English universities and public schools in order to provoke interest in the conversion of India.

Returning home in 1808, he did a great deal by his powerful sermons to rouse enthusiasm for missions in the East.

The most famous of " Simeon's men," Henry Martyn, reached Calcutta in May 1806, having witnessed, on the way out, the capture of the Cape of Good Hope from the Dutch. Senior Wrangler, First Smith's Prizeman and Fellow of St. John's College, Cambridge, he was a man of saintly character and intense zeal, who in six brief years of service burned himself out for God, leaving an imperishable memory to his own and subsequent generations. From Bengal he went to Cawnpore, and thence into Persia, dying at Tokat in 1812. There followed him to India his Cambridge contemporary and close friend, Daniel Corrie, destined one day to be Bishop of Madras; and, a few years later, inspired like the others by Simeon, and also by Martyn himself, " that good, serene, diligent person," Thomas Thomason. These five chaplains—Brown, Buchanan, Martyn, Corrie and Thomason—and the work they did, played an essential part in preparing the way for the revision of the E.I.C. Charter.

Wilberforce, whose speech in Parliament, in June 1813, marked the climax of the successful agitation, declared that " this cause of the recognition of our Christian obligation to British India was the greatest he had lived for, not even excepting the emancipation of the slaves."[1] It had been an exacting struggle for the newly established missionary societies, and most of all for the Baptists, who were by choice its storm centre. The winter of 1812-13, when numerous petitions were being signed and Christian opinion brought to

[1] Quoted by S. Pearce Carey, *William Carey*, 8th edition, p. 331.

expression on the Charter issue in a variety of ways, was the winter of Napoleon's retreat from Moscow. In April 1813, Josiah Pratt's *Missionary Register*, then in its first year, contained an article with the topical title " India secured to Britain by Russian victories."

### III

The repercussions of the Napoleonic struggle and the general war temper combined to delay the opening of India to missionary work. Meantime, in its attempts to begin the evangelization of the South Seas, the L.M.S. had been hindered in quite different fashion.

Immediately after its foundation in 1795, the new Society eagerly responded to the enthusiastic pleas of Thomas Haweis, and organized an elaborate expedition to Tahiti. The *Duff* was purchased for £4,800, and a Captain James Wilson volunteered to sail her to the South Seas. He was a remarkable man, whose earlier life had been full of hair-raising adventures and hair-breadth escapes in India and elsewhere. The missionary party consisted of thirty men, together with a number of wives and children; one of them, Mrs Eyre, was sixty-four years old. Only four of the men were ordained, the rest being craftsmen and tradesmen. The vessel started down the Thames on August 10th, 1796. Haweis remained on board as far as Spithead. There it was necessary to seek a convoy, because of the war between France and England. The first was missed, and there was a tedious wait of six weeks till the next. The Atlantic was successfully crossed and South America sighted. Captain Wilson then tried to negotiate Cape Horn, but decided that it was too risky, and that he had better sail eastwards again, via South

Africa and Australia, though that meant doubling the distance. Tahiti was not reached till March 1797, and the first difficult years of establishing a missionary settlement in the midst of a primitive heathen people then began. Captain Cook had suggested that the islands had a population of about 200,000. It was soon estimated by the missionaries at no more than 16,000. Two other small settlements were established, the one 1,200 miles north-west of Tahiti, on one of the Friendly Islands, the other on the Marquesas. At the end of the year the *Duff* returned to England.

Enthusiasm and interest were growing, and a second expedition was at once organized. It sailed from London in December 1798. Two months later, off Rio de Janeiro, the ship was captured by a French raider. The missionary party, which had in it many women and children, was split up and taken, some in prize vessels, some in *Le Grand Buonaparte* itself, to Montevideo on the River Plate. There the French sold the *Duff*, but offered the missionaries one of their other ships in exchange for bills on the Society. There was some talk of trying to get to the west coast of Africa to start a mission there. At last an arrangement was made to take the whole party to Rio de Janeiro, the crew of the *Duff* working a vessel purchased by some Portuguese from the French. On June 5th, 1799, after four weeks of most unpleasant battling with contrary winds, this ship was intercepted by the Portuguese fleet. The missionaries were divided into three parties, and on board three of the vessels of the fleet were taken to Lisbon. Thence, without more delay, but in the face of considerable danger of renewed capture by the French, most of them made their way back to England, arriving there in October. One of the missionaries had to stay behind in Lisbon, owing to the illness of his wife, who died there; on his way home, he was captured by a French raider, then recaptured by a Guernsey cutter, and finally reached Plymouth in January 1800.

It is hardly surprising that, after so many months of hardship and peril, most of the party became convinced that God did not desire them to serve Him in the South Seas. The Directors of the L.M.S., however, felt their responsibilities to those already in Tahiti and the other islands, and were no more willing to be turned aside from their missionary purpose than were the B.M.S. leaders when faced with the opposition of the East India Company. Though the loss of the *Duff* and the supplies she carried was estimated at £10,000, the L.M.S. made arrangements for a third party to set out in the *Royal Admiral*, a ship engaged in carrying convicts to Botany Bay. The missionary band consisted of twelve men, four of whom had been on the *Duff* on her second, ill-fated trip; they reached Tahiti in July 1801. Another five years passed before the next consignment of letters and stores arrived, and only then because of the generous and energetic action of Samuel Marsden, the Government chaplain of Sydney; communications and goods from England had accumulated at Port Jackson, and he finally chartered a special sloop to take them to Tahiti.

Two posts in ten years! Completely cut off from home and friends, the missionaries had been through many grievous and disheartening experiences. The realities of heathenism in the South Seas proved very different from the rather idealized descriptions of Captain Cook. Of the Friendly Islands' party three were killed by the natives within two years. On Tahiti, within three months, three of the first band of women died. A number of the missionary party took the earliest opportunity of making their way to Australia; and it is to the honour of Mrs Eyre that she remained at her post, though deserted by all the other women. One of the ordained men " went native." When the *Royal Admiral* at length arrived in 1801, there were only seven of the original group on Tahiti. Five years later, when letters were next sent home, there were still no conversions to report, and in the subsequent months conditions grew much worse. Wars and rebellions on the island compelled the withdrawal of almost all the missionaries. The L.M.S. Directors were actually considering the abandonment of the mission, when the young Tahiti chief, Pomare, asked for Christian baptism. This was followed, in 1815, by the overthrow of idolatry in the island. A new era had at last begun, and, as if to emphasize the fact, there reached the neighbouring island of Eimeo, in November 1817, the bold, restless, glowing John Williams, who was to sail tirelessly among the islands of the South Seas, opening them up to the Gospel, till his martyr-death on Erromanga more than twenty years later.

The *Duff* was captured in February 1799. The event gave a fillip to the already keen interest of the friends of the L.M.S. in religious conditions in France. The overthrow of papal authority there seemed to open the way for fruitful evangelistic work. In 1801 £200 was appropriated from the Society's funds for the distribution of Testaments, Bibles and tracts among the numerous French and Dutch prisoners of war who were then in England; and as soon as the Treaty of Amiens was concluded David Bogue and Joseph Hardcastle hastened over to Paris, and laid plans for important new L.M.S. agencies throughout France. The renewal of the war, after a truce of only a few months, brought these good purposes to naught, but they show that generation grasping every opportunity in the interests of the cause it had at heart. The leaders and their supporters were undeterred and unembittered by what had been done by their country's enemies. One of the most interesting early gifts to the L.M.S. was £18 16s. from a group of seamen on board H.M.S. *Bellerophon*, " being the first division of their prize money arising from the victory obtained over the French fleet off Egypt on August 1st, 1798, under the command of Lord Nelson."

IV

When news of the capture of the *Duff* reached London, the Church Missionary Society voted one hundred guineas to the L.M.S. as a mark of sympathy. The C.M.S. was then but a few months old, and the gesture was the more significant and welcome as the new Society had been founded because of a deep desire on the part of its promoters to remain true in their missionary work to the principles of Anglican Church-order. Recognizing the special interest of the S.P.G. in the British plantations in America and the West Indies, and that there was as yet no official permission for missionary work in India, the C.M.S. had set itself the task of sending missionaries " to the Continent of Africa, or the other parts of the heathen world." It had to find men, money and openings for mission stations.

The greatest difficulty proved to be the finding of men, and it is a memory specially worth treasuring at the present time that the earliest agents of the C.M.S. were Germans. Evangelical clergymen throughout England had been written to with a view to discovering whether they knew of any likely candidates, but in vain. Even Charles Simeon could as yet find none in Cambridge. Help came by way of Dr C. F. A. Steinkopff, one of the most picturesque figures in the religious life of London in those days. A young man of twenty-eight, handsome, winning in manner and eloquent, he had but recently arrived as pastor of the German Lutheran Church in the Savoy. He was quickly and warmly received into evangelical circles, both Anglican and Nonconformist, and soon showed himself a great asset in the many new enterprises that were on foot. He was appointed one of the foreign secretaries of the R.T.S.; he was present when the Bible Society was founded, making one of the most decisive of the speeches, and was at once elected one of the three secretaries, he representing the foreign Protestant churches, and Joseph Hughes and Josiah Pratt being his colleagues. Till his resignation in 1826, Steinkopff was indefatigable in the service of the Bible Society, furthering its interests in every possible way, interviewing foreign potentates and undertaking arduous continental journeys. He was present at the Jubilee celebrations of the Bible Society in 1853, a venerable figure, eighty years old, and the only surviving member of the original committee.

His service to the C.M.S. in the matter of candidates must have been one of Steinkopff's earliest activities on his arrival in London as a young man. He was able to tell of a missionary seminary established in Berlin, one of the final flowerings of the Pietist movement, formed in part because of reports of the L.M.S. venturings, and destined to supply candidates both to that Society and to the C.M.S. Following correspondence between Josiah Pratt and the head of the Berlin Seminary, two young Germans reached England in November 1802. At their first meeting with the committee there was no way of conversing with them, and the business had to be adjourned till Steinkopff could be present as translator. They were accepted as " missionary catechists " for West Africa, and were sent to stay in Clapham, where one of them fell in love with the governess in John Venn's household. After discussion, it seemed well that they should receive full Lutheran orders, and accordingly they went back to Germany for ordination, and were finally valedicted in London in January 1804.

New difficulties then arose. How could they be conveyed to Africa? Napoleon was threatening the invasion of England. The only vessel that could at first be heard of was a slave-ship, fitted up for the trade which Wilberforce was energetically denouncing. They could hardly be sent in that. Zachary Macaulay at length secured passages in the *John*, which belonged to a firm of woollen drapers, and with the help of an armed convoy she got the new missionaries safely to Sierra Leone. A second party of three Germans, who sailed in February 1806, after five weeks of waiting in Liverpool, were stranded on the Irish coast, and had to stay there for nearly two months. They started again at last, this time from Bristol, but had to put in to Falmouth to join a convoy. The captain of their vessel started suddenly without them, and they would have been left behind altogether had not contrary winds driven the whole fleet back to port. On the next attempt, their vessel lost the convoy, and narrowly escaped capture by a French raider on its way to Madeira. There the captain died, and the ship was detained for three more weary months. Not till the end of September did they reach Sierra Leone.

The adventures of the third party of men from Berlin are thus described in the C.M.S. Report: " These brethren left Berlin on July 2nd, 1807, embracing the opportunity afforded between the time of signing the armistice between the Russians and the French, and the conclusion of the Peace of Tilsit. By avoiding the great roads and travelling on foot, they arrived without interruption, through many difficulties, at Wernigerode. From Wernigerode they went to Altona; from that place to Tonningen, and thence they embarked for this country."[1]

By the time this third party arrived in England, the C.M.S. had faced—as the B.M.S. and L.M.S. had already had to do—the question of training their recruits, whether they came from the Continent or from the home churches. Most of the Baptist candidates in the early years were instructed either by Carey's friend, John Sutcliff, of Olney, or at the Bristol Baptist College. David Bogue undertook at Gosport the preparation of those who were to serve the L.M.S. It was Thomas Scott who added to his many other labours the training of C.M.S. candidates. Although, in 1802, Henry Martyn had, under Simeon's influence, been in touch with the C.M.S. as a possible candidate, it was only by taking an E.I.C. chaplaincy that it seemed possible for him to get to India, the land on which his heart was set. For long no other Englishman volunteered to the C.M.S., and when at last in 1809 two candidates were forthcoming, they were not from the universities, but a Carlisle joiner and an Oxfordshire shoemaker. They offered to go out as " lay settlers " among the Maoris of New Zealand. In late 1828 Macaulay noted that while the life of the missionary

[1] Stock, i. pp. 86-7.

martyr might be admired, not ten of the ten thousand English clergymen had thought for a moment of engaging in it.[1]

It was not the privileged who came forward for this new enterprise, in spite of the example set by the Clapham Sect. Those whose offers were accepted during the next few years had had few early advantages, and they joined fresh parties of Germans at Scott's Buckinghamshire rectory. A curate who volunteered wanted £700 a year if he went to Africa, and this the committee naturally declined. The spirit Melvill Horne had castigated was unfortunately still abroad. In the first fifteen years of the C.M.S. twenty-four missionaries were sent abroad, seventeen of whom were Germans. It was 1815 before the first English graduate found a place on the Society's roll. Only after many disappointments could two bishops be discovered willing to ordain two others of the candidates. Also in 1815, the year of Waterloo, three single women volunteered, ready to go anywhere in any capacity. Their application was supported by the E.I.C. chaplain, Daniel Corrie, who was in England at the time. Difficult as it was, however, to get recruits, the C.M.S. committee was not yet ready to send unmarried women abroad, unless they were going out to join brothers who were already in missionary service.

V

Formidable indeed were the obstacles placed in the way of the societies by the attitude of the East India Company, by the hazards of war and of slow and scanty communication, and by the difficulty of obtaining recruits. The faith and philanthropy of that generation

[1] Essay on Hallam, *Edinburgh Review*.

proved costly, and only men of great resource and strong conviction could have persisted in their endeavours. Many other notable stories come from the records of the Napoleonic decades.

There is, for example, the tale of Samuel Marsden, already mentioned as the Port Jackson friend of the L.M.S. missionaries in Tahiti. A Yorkshire boy who had started life as a blacksmith, he was adopted for training as a clergyman and, in 1793, while still an undergraduate at Cambridge, accepted appointment as the second chaplain to Botany Bay, New South Wales, whither the Government was shipping convicts. But for the pleas of Wilberforce and his friends, the penal settlement would probably have been left without any religious ministration. The life of David Brainerd was Marsden's inspiration, and for more than forty years he laboured heroically in a situation of great loneliness and difficulty, not only doing fine work of a varied character in New South Wales, but also gaining the proud title of " apostle of New Zealand " by his ceaseless concern for the evangelization of the Maoris. Even after he had persuaded the C.M.S. to send Hall and King out as " lay settlers," it long proved impossible to get them from Botany Bay to New Zealand. The traders and political agents openly stated, that if they could not continue the exploitation of the natives, then they would rather see them exterminated. Every possible obstacle was put in Marsden's way, and the vilest slanders were circulated about him. The early years of the New Zealand mission were filled with grim and terrible disappointments and cruelties. Through them all Marsden held to his missionary purpose, resourceful and undespairing, and it is not too much to say that " the very existence of the now flourishing Dominion of New Zealand is due to his courage and faith."[1]

There is the story of John Vanderkemp, full of unexpected changes, and possible perhaps only in days as confused and troubled as those of Napoleon. He was born in 1747 at Rotterdam, the son of a Dutch Lutheran minister. After studying medicine, he entered the army, showing considerable skill as an officer, but living a wild life. When he was thirty, he fell deeply in love with a young Leyden spinner of humble circumstances but fine character, and she proved willing to take both him and an illegitimate daughter. On his marriage, he left the army and came to Edinburgh, and after two years' study there secured a doctor's degree. Returning to Holland, he set up in practice. Vanderkemp was for long a rather arrogant deist, though sincerely perplexed about certain philosophical and theological issues. Then, in 1791, came a tragic boating accident on the Meuse, in which his wife and daughter were drowned and he barely escaped. It led to a profound change in his spiritual outlook and temper, and to an over-whelming desire to serve God. The outbreak of war in Europe drew him back into the army for a time, but in 1795, while at a loose end, waiting, as he put it, " for the wink of Providence," he read the accounts of the founding of the L.M.S., and before many months had passed had offered himself, a man of nearly fifty, for the new enterprise. His Dutch background, his medical experience and his knowledge of English seemed clearly to fit him for the leadership of the projected mission to South Africa. After helping to

[1] Cf. Stock, i. p. 209. Viscount Bledisloe in his foreword to *Peacemaker of the Tribes*, 1939, applies words very similar to these to Henry Williams, who was in New Zealand itself from 1823-67. Marsden went across seven times from New South Wales between 1814 and 1837. See below, p. 123.

found the Netherlands Missionary Society, he therefore set out, with three companions, for the colony at the Cape, which was half English and half Dutch. They had to travel in a convict ship which was bound for Australia, and for part of the way the *Duff*—then starting on her second disastrous journey—was in the same convoy. Arriving at last in Cape Town, the missionaries found themselves in the midst of racial and national strife. Vanderkemp set out at once for the wilds of Kaffirland, and then, unable to find any permanent centre for missionary work, and in spite of the strong opposition of the colonists, went on among the despised and downtrodden Hottentots. At Bethelsdorp, near Port Elizabeth, he established a famous missionary settlement, and for the remaining ten years of his life was the brave and tireless champion of the natives.

"It was his distinctive achievement that, believing in the Gospel of Christ as a universal principle, he so preached it and by many an act of pity and love so embodied it, as to erect a challenging standard before his fellow-Europeans, both Dutch and British —a higher moral standard than they had visualized before."[1]

Or, turning to another part of the world, there is the memorable story of Adoniram Judson and his heroic wife—pioneers in Burma. Judson was one of the little group of American students at Andover who, in 1810, asked to be sent as missionaries to Africa. It was the reading of one of the sermons of Claudius Buchanan, the E.I.C. chaplain, that had first stirred the young man's soul. The American Board of Commissioners

[1] A. D. Martin, *Doctor Vanderkemp*, p. 194.

for Foreign Missions came into existence to send out the volunteers, a body supported by Congregationalists and Presbyterians and by those who belonged to the Dutch and German Reformed Churches. Judson was sent to England to make contact with the L.M.S. His ship was captured by a French privateer, and Judson was imprisoned for a time with the sailors in the hold, and later in Bayonne, under conditions of great hardship. He escaped to England, and after returning to America set out from there to India. On the voyage he and his wife adopted Baptist views. They reached Serampore in 1812, when, as already indicated, the missionaries there were having considerable difficulties with the authorities. Carey could only advise the Americans to seek some other sphere of labour. After a short stay in Mauritius, they made their way to Rangoon. For thirty-seven years Judson laboured in Burma, under conditions that would have overwhelmed any but the bravest. During the war between the East India Company and the independent Burmese monarch, he and other foreigners suffered the horrors of imprisonment in a loathsome oriental jail for twenty-one months, but he lived to lay the foundations of one of the strongest Christian communities anywhere in Asia.

Or again, there is the story of Robert Morrison's attempts to prepare the way for entry into the closed land of China. It is said to have been Joseph Hardcastle who suggested to the L.M.S. that a mission should be started in the Far East. This was in 1804, the year of Napoleon's threatened invasion. Only one British subject was supposed then to know the Chinese language, but the Directors of the L.M.S., in spite of their other preoccupations, realized, as did Carey and Marshman

at Serampore, how much might be accomplished could
the Bible be translated and got into China. Morrison
was a Northumberland youth. After a time of study
under David Bogue, he made his way alone, via
America, first to Canton, and then to Macao, which was
Portuguese territory and where the East India Company
had a factory. In Bengal the authorities were still
vigorously resisting missionary work. Farther east
conditions were somewhat different, and the E.I.C.
was glad of Morrison's services as Chinese translator.
This rendered his position as a resident secure, provided
him with a good salary, and gave him freedom for his
Bible translation. He spent his strength in incessant
literary toil. After a few years, realizing the uncertain-
ties of life in the small European concessions on the
Chinese coast, he conceived the plan of a missionary
settlement at Malacca, where workers might be trained
and where the many Chinese colonists could be
evangelized. Morrison's bold scheme, which embraced
the whole of the East Indies and the China coast, came
to be known as the Ultra-Ganges Mission. Its early and
very successful development was largely in the hands of
William Milne, a man of unusual gifts, great force of
character and intense spirituality, who had reached
Morrison as colleague in 1813. Until 1842, this
mission, with its centres in Batavia, Penang and
Singapore, provided almost the only means of direct
contact with the Chinese. When, a year or so before
his death, after a quarter of a century of toil, Morrison
reviewed what had been accomplished, he had to
confess: " Only ten persons have been baptized." But
the Chinese Bible was already beginning to do its work.
" He built the bridge over which a great army has since

passed to greater victories than he dared even to dream of."[1]

Any age might be proud of men like these. Of intrepid spirit, they were ready for the most heroic self-sacrifice in order to translate their purposes into deeds.

[1] J. C. Harris, *Couriers of Christ*, p. 101.

# CHAPTER VI

# THE NINETEENTH-CENTURY ACHIEVEMENT

" Missions are, in spite of many faults, a standing protest against self-indulgence, cynicism, and vanity. Take away foreign missions from the recent history of Britain, and you would have robbed that history of its purest glory. No one can have any knowledge of religious society in this country without knowing how noble, unselfish, and courageous is the enthusiasm which carries to the end of the earth young men and women to whom life in Britain is rich in promise. They go forth under no illusions, for the records of their predecessors are before them, and those records are eloquent of privation and death. They consecrate with their graves the desperate wastes and pestilential swamps of Africa, the bleak solitudes of Polynesia, the ice-bound plains where the Esquimaux wander, the plague-haunted purlieus of Oriental cities. Those graves perish quickly, the rank vegetation of the tropics or the all-obliterating snow shrouds them from sight; but the tradition of heroism does not perish. It flows ever through the nation, swollen by a thousand contributions of personal service, a stream of holy and gracious influences, fertilizing character, and beautifying life." H. Hensley Henson, *Christian Morality*, Gifford Lectures, 1935-6. O.U.P., 1941, p. 245.

I

THE HOPES of those who founded the missionary societies during the tumultuous years of the Napoleonic struggle were high. The first agents were men of daring and endurance. But that generation would indeed have been amazed could it have witnessed the expansion of the Christian Church during the nineteenth century which came as a direct consequence of its pioneering efforts. So rapid and extensive was the growth that there is little doubt that it exceeded that of any other century in the long history of the Church. With gathering momentum the frontiers of Christendom were carried into the very centres of heathenism abroad, and its fellowship was transformed from one that was almost exclusively European and American into one that embraced those of every continent and race.

In the tables which Carey prepared for his *Enquiry*, in the columns headed " Religion," the one word " pagans " had to be set down against more than seventy of the areas mentioned. In many more cases the entry ran, " Pagans and Papists," or " Pagans and a few Christians," where the Dutch are usually meant. How different was the situation after the lapse of a century! It is estimated that, connected with the non-Roman missionary bodies, whose origins we have been considering, there were in Asia, by the beginning of the twentieth century, 600,000 communicant Church members, a native leadership of 38,000 and more than 8,000 European missionaries. In Africa, where the scramble for colonies was only just over, there were some 340,000 Church members, 22,000 trained African leaders and more than 3,000 missionaries. In the scattered areas of Australasia and the South Seas, there were only 700 missionaries, but the Church membership was more than 110,000, and there were 5,000 native leaders, while in Latin America and the West Indies, Churches with 130,000 members had a native staff of 6,000 and a foreign missionary staff of 1,400. That meant, in all, a communicant membership of not far short of a million and a quarter, with its own trained leadership of 70,000 and a missionary company of more than 14,000.[1]

Figures like these must, of course, be set against the population totals of the different areas, and, particularly in China, where so large a proportion of the vast human family is to be found, they seem of relatively little importance, unless one keeps in mind, first, the small and hazardous beginnings of this modern expansion of the Church, secondly, the immensity of the task which was attempted, and thirdly, the remarkable influence achieved, in all parts of the world, by these sometimes tiny and isolated yet often virile Christian communities. A just appraisal of what was done in the nineteenth century must recognize these things, and note also how few were the areas into which no entry at all had been secured by the end of the Victorian era.

At the World Missionary Conference, held at Edinburgh in 1910, a special survey was made of the " Unoccupied Sections of the World."[2] Attention was drawn to certain great areas which were almost untouched: in Asia, Manchuria, Mongolia, Turkestan, Tibet, Afghanistan, and (save for Roman missions) Indo-China; and in Africa, the large region bordering the Sahara, large parts of both East and West Africa, and of the Congo Basin. To these places had to be added Arabia and Syria and considerable districts of the Malay Peninsula. It was estimated that some 122,000,000 people were without any missionary provision whatever, because, it was suggested, of the

[1] Figures from the *Interpretative Statistical Survey of the World Mission of the Christian Church*, 1938. It is of interest to note that between 1800 and 1900 the population of the United States increased almost twelvefold, and the membership of the Evangelical Churches no less than thirty-eightfold. See E. E. White, *The Story of Missions*, New York, 1926, p. 140.

[2] *Edinburgh Conference Report*, i. pp. 279-88.

isolation and difficulty of access of most of these regions, serious political hindrances in many cases and lack of an adequate and comprehensive vision on the part of the Christian forces. The amazing thing, however, is not that these areas remained unentered, but that it could seriously be claimed that a real beginning had been made in almost every other land. A hundred years earlier there was still no direct entry for missionaries into British India, the door into China and Japan was fast closed, while Africa was a dark unexplored continent.

II

The creation of this new world-wide Christian fellowship—perhaps the most significant achievement of the nineteenth century, and certainly worthy to be set beside the remarkable scientific progress of the age—is quite beyond adequate portrayal in a few pages. It was a complex movement, vast in its extent and influence, but it was the direct consequence of the vision and devotion which we have been considering in the previous chapters. The missionary societies were formed, as we have seen, by small groups of men, who challenged the indifference and hostility of their contemporaries. The beginnings seemed to the outsider unimpressive and hazardous, if not foolish. During the nineteenth century, however, these societies increased enormously in size and strength and in the range of their activities. New associations were formed, in Britain, on the continent of Europe and in America. No longer the concern of only small coteries of missionaries and enthusiasts, the cause of world evangelism secured widespread popular support.

Dr S. C. Carpenter, attempting to indicate the

advance of the Anglican communion during the
hundred years which followed the French Revolution,
has to confess that its limits are " in themselves as
baffling to the chronicler, as inexhaustible and, indeed,
as unreachable, as those which confronted the writer of
the Epistle to the Hebrews."[1] By the end of the nineteenth century the C.M.S. had hundreds of missionaries at work in many lands and continents, and an
annual income of £300,000. The older Anglican
societies, the S.P.C.K. and the S.P.G., had revived and
expanded, and were engaged in important new enterprises. The S.P.G., in particular, had developed its
distinctly missionary activities in impressive fashion.
Its interest was no longer confined to the British
Empire or to British subjects; its service had become
world-wide.[2] The M.M.S., which carried on the
tradition of Thomas Coke, greatly extended the work
he had begun in the West Indies and was able to set up
there a self-governing Methodist Conference with a
communicant membership of some 50,000; work in
Ceylon and India had steadily developed; in West
Africa and South Africa heroic pioneering began to bear
rich fruit, and missionaries were also sent to the South
Seas, to China and to many other parts. The B.M.S.,
by the time its centenary was reached, had more than
170 missionaries, half of them in India, where Carey
and Thomas had with such difficulty begun the work,
and the rest in China, Central Africa, the West Indies
and Europe; its first collection of £13 2s. 6d., made in
Andrew Fuller's snuff-box, had grown to an annual
income of over £70,000. The L.M.S. had, in 1895, an

[1] *Church and People, 1789-1889*, p. 434.
[2] Ibid., p. 428: " The life of the S.P.G. has always been a normal part
of the life of the Church, sharing its virtues and its defects. And the most
glorious period of the history of the S.P.G. has been since 1889."

income of £150,000, employed in vigorous missionary enterprises in the South Seas and in India, Africa and China, and the names of not a few of its missionaries had become household words throughout Christendom. The Church of Scotland was engaged in very substantial missionary tasks in different parts of India and Africa, in Jamaica, in Manchuria and in the New Hebrides. The Bible Society and its associated enterprises had extended their scope to every continent, and the list of languages in which translations had appeared was already of bewildering length.

The century saw the birth of many new societies. The Irish Presbyterians, the Welsh Calvinistic Methodists and the English Presbyterians followed the example of the Church of Scotland. The General Baptists and the Strict Baptists, as well as the different groups of Methodists, and before long the Society of Friends (1865) all set up their own associations for carrying on missionary work abroad. The stream of societies formed during the Napoleonic struggle widened out into a great flood of Christian activity overseas. New areas claimed attention and were specially provided for, as, for example, South America (1844) and Melanesia (1848). An attempt was made to deal with particular needs, as in the case of the Colonial Bishoprics' Fund (1841), in which Gladstone took a deep personal interest. Whilst not strictly a missionary foundation, it was generously supported by the S.P.G. and the S.P.C.K., and helped greatly in the growth and organization of the Anglican communion throughout the British Empire and its dependencies, the ten overseas dioceses of 1841 becoming no less than eighty-two by 1891.[1]

[1] See W. F. France, *The Oversea Episcopate*, 1941.

On the Continent a notable series of missionary organizations came into existence. The Basel Evangelical Missionary Society (1815) and the Paris Society for Evangelical Missions (1822) were the first to be formed; by the middle of the century seven important German societies had been organized, and by 1860 the Swedish, Norwegian, Dutch and Finnish Churches had their own missionary agencies. In America the growth of missionary societies was no less remarkable. American Christians had to face three formidable tasks at home; first, that of evangelizing the settlements that moved ever farther westwards towards the Pacific, then that of ministering to the incoming millions from Europe, and thirdly, that of meeting the older complex problems connected with the Red Indians and the negroes. In addition to meeting these demands, very considerable and successful missionary enterprises were undertaken in other parts of the world, notably in Japan, in Central and South America, and in the Middle East.

How rapidly Christian sentiment changed may be seen from the fact that in 1843, just fifty years after Carey and Thomas ran the gauntlet into India, and Horne put the finishing touches to his urgent appeal, a Church of England divine chose as the subject of his Bampton Lectures in Oxford University *The Past and Prospective Extension of the Gospel by Missions to the Heathen*.

The year 1858 has been described as the *annus mirabilis* of nineteenth-century missionary history. Simultaneously, in four great areas of the world, hindrances to evangelistic enterprise were removed, and the Church was free to advance. In Africa, there were the important explorations and discoveries of

Speke, Burton and Livingstone. In India, the privileged rule of the East India Company came to an end. The Treaty of Tientsin opened the door into China, and at the same time the way into Japan became clear through the Treaty of Yedo. These events caused a new outburst of missionary interest and zeal. The Universities' Mission to Central Africa (1859), for example, resulted from Livingstone's stirring appeals, and a few years later Hudson Taylor organized the justly famous China Inland Mission (1865).

Already special organizations had been formed for developing both women's and medical work. The Napoleonic generation had not been ready for single-women missionaries, save in a very few cases when they accompanied their brothers, or taught in schools connected with some missionary settlement. As late as 1842, Bishop Wilson wrote from Calcutta that he objected " on principle " to a single woman being sent out to India. " I imagine," he wrote, " the beloved Persis, Tryphena and Tryphosa, Julia, Nereus and his sister, and others who ' laboured much in the Lord,' remained in their own neighbourhoods and families, and that no unmarried female would have thought of a voyage of fourteen thousand miles to find out a scene of duty. The whole thing is against the Apostolic maxim ' I suffer not a woman to speak in the Church.' "[1] But the debt of those of the pioneering generations to their wives is beyond all telling, as Bishop Wilson himself would have been the first to admit. Women were found ready to go out with their husbands to strange lands, enduring the utmost hardship and contributing far more than has ever been adequately

[1] See P. L. Garlick, " A Century of Progress in Women's Work," *The Church Overseas*, July 1934.

recognized to the breaking down of suspicion and hostility and the gradual upbuilding of a Christian community. In many cases, women with the flame of missionary zeal alight in their hearts were willing to be sent abroad to be the partners of men whom they had not previously known. Something of the attitude of the early decades of the nineteenth century in these matters may be seen in Charlotte Brontë's *Jane Eyre*, which was published in 1847. St John Rivers, it may be remembered, does his best to persuade Jane to go with him to India. Mary Kingsley once wrote of missionaries' wives as " one heroic form of human being whose praise has never been adequately sung."[1] She had seen with her own eyes many of those who had braved the dangers of West Africa.

The story of the sad mental breakdown of Carey's wife is well known. The first woman to go out under the C.M.S. also had a tragic time. She had been governess in the house of John Venn, of Clapham, and married one of the first German recruits. He turned out badly. She had to leave him, and for some years he led a wandering life on the west coast of Africa. Later he was taken back into the service of the C.M.S. as a translator, and his wife agreed to go out again to him. It was not long, however, before she died of fever.

We may take as more typical the story of Anna Hinderer. Born in Norfolk in 1827, she had spent several years in the home of the Vicar of Lowestoft, whose wife was a sister of Elizabeth Fry. It was natural that she should there become deeply interested in the developing work of the C.M.S., and she came early to feel that a missionary calling was to be hers. She was introduced to David Hinderer, one of the

[1] See Stephen Gwynn, *Life of Mary Kingsley*, p. 72.

Germans serving in West Africa with the C.M.S., and went out with him in 1852 to the Yoruba country, north of Lagos. They were pioneers in Ibadan, and for seventeen years braved fevers and other severe illnesses, first one colleague and then another succumbing to the climate. For nearly five years they were almost completely cut off from friends at the coast by fierce inter-tribal warfare. Anna Hinderer's journals and letters[1] tell a moving story of faithful devotion, and their intensity—reminiscent in many ways of that of David Brainerd—can be understood better when it is realized that the writer knew well that any week might be her last. Her story was that of many another woman, save that she had no children of her own. Instead, first in the native mud dwelling where she had to live, and then in the newly built mission house, she cared for eight or ten African children, playing an essential part in laying the foundations of the Christian Church in that needy area.

It was during the lifetime of Anna Hinderer that the way was opened for single-women missionaries. " The Society for Promoting Female Education in the East " was formed in London in 1834 as the result of the appeal of an American missionary who had worked in China, and three years later a similar society was organized in Scotland. At first they met with much opposition, but before many decades had passed all the larger missionary bodies had their own special " Women's Auxiliary." By the end of the century a very large number of women missionaries were at work abroad. It might indeed be claimed that it was in the

---

[1] *Seventeen Years in the Yoruba Country. Memorials of Anna Hinderer*, 1872. There is a description of the Lowestoft vicar and his wife in Percy Lubbock's *Earlham*.

field of missionary service that single women first clearly demonstrated, by their achievements and by their heroism and self-sacrifice, their right to full emancipation.

Organized medical work owed its origin, as did women's work, to the visit of an American missionary to Britain. Peter Parker, who " opened the gates of China with a lancet when European cannon could not heave a single bar,"[1] spoke so effectively that the Edinburgh Medical Missionary Society was formed in 1841, and during the second half of the nineteenth century medical work was developed in many different parts of the world, though it is only the twentieth century that has seen the value of medical missions thoroughly appreciated.

### III

These striking developments meant that what was regarded as a strange and unattractive, nay even pernicious, enthusiasm in 1800 had, a century later, become an accepted channel of Christian witness and philanthropy. It must not, of course, be thought of as completely uninterrupted progress. Interest waxed and waned. Certain periods were marked by greater activity and conviction than others. Taken as a whole, however, the century saw a spectacular growth and consolidation of missionary work, and the closing decade witnessed a noteworthy new outburst of zeal and the formation of not a few additional missionary organizations. Moreover, this mighty outflow of life from the Churches of Northern Europe and America was paralleled in the Roman Catholic Church in renewed activity and devotion on a large scale. The

[1] Quoted by C. C. Chesterman, *In the Service of Suffering*, p. 14.

words of Dr Kraemer are no whit too strong. " The awakening since the eighteenth century of the missionary spirit in the Church is one of the most amazing movements in the history of the world."[1]

In the lands overseas it was a century of great pioneering figures, men and women of truly apostolic stature, who blazed the trail into new territories, facing great hardships and often labouring many years before any converts were won.[2] A calendar of names, though they be of the bravest, may seem dull and prosaic, yet very little knowledge and imagination are needed to make one realize how truly remarkable a succession are the more famous missionary personalities of the nineteenth century.

We have already had glimpses of Carey, Marshman and Ward, the notable trio who directed from Serampore such manifold and fruitful missionary enterprises; of heroic Judson and his wife at work in Burma; of Marsden in Australia and New Zealand; of Vanderkemp, the Dutchman who gave his life for the Hottentots and the Bushmen ; of Morrison, preparing for a renewed assault on China. These were all sons of the eighteenth century, and they set out on their tasks long before the overthrow of Napoleon. To the same generation belonged Reginald Heber—rector and squire, poet and scholar—who spent the last three years of his life, from 1823 to 1826, as Bishop of Calcutta, and whose statesmanship and devotion to the missionary cause did much to arouse the Church of England to her responsibilities.[3] Another of that generation was John

[1] *The Christian Message in a Non-Christian World*, p. 34.

[2] Cf. *Rethinking Missions*, p. 289. " The history of Protestant missions is a story of the influence of personality upon individuals and communities."

[3] His well-known hymn *From Greenland's icy mountains* should be compared with those referred to in Chapter IV.

Philip, born the year of the outbreak of the American War of Independence, who left a church in Aberdeen that he might go out to South Africa for the L.M.S., at a time when there was acute tension between the white and black populations; he spent thirty years fighting for the rights of the natives—Wilberforce and Buxton helping him in England—and it is now recognized that " in a just view John Philip must rank high among the Makers of South Africa."[1] Nor should young John Smith, of Demerara, be forgotten; for seven years he worked among the negroes of the sugar plantations, enduring the bitter hostility of his fellow-countrymen. He died in 1824 while in prison under sentence of death on the charge of having spread discontent among the slaves. The case made a deep impression in Britain and was the subject of a lengthy debate in the House of Commons. It played an important part in helping forward the movement for the abolition of slavery.

The next generation consisted of men who were born while Britain was actively menaced by Bonaparte, those whose childhood was enlivened by frightening stories of the threatened French invasion, but who heard also stirring accounts of missionary adventurings in India and the South Seas. They form an impressive company, these children of a century and a half ago— John Wilson, of Bombay, and Alexander Duff, of Calcutta, men of learning and statesmanship in the presentation of the Gospel to the Hindus, the former especially notable for his interest in female education and his emphasis on the study of the native languages, the latter remarkably successful in interesting the Indian

[1] W. M. McMillan, *The Cape Colour Question*, 1927, p. 108. Cf. E. A. Walker, *History of South Africa*, 1937 (2nd ed.) p. 158.

intelligentsia in the traditions of Western Christendom;
Henry Williams, who, after ten years' exciting service
in the Navy, volunteered to go out to the hardships and
dangers of New Zealand, and there spent forty-four
years as a peacemaker among the wild Maori tribes;
John Williams, the shipbuilder missionary of the South
Seas, who was killed and eaten by the natives of the
New Hebrides in retaliation, it is believed, for the
cruelties previously perpetrated there by the crew of a
trading ship; and then the great Bishop Selwyn, of New
Zealand and Melanesia—versatile, courageous, energetic and influential both in Britain and Australasia;
Robert Moffat, born the year the L.M.S. was founded,
who laboured for half a century in Bechuanaland, and
David Jones, the leader in the early stormy but
glorious years of the Church in Madagascar; fiery
young William Knibb, the champion of the Jamaica
slaves, and gaunt Alfred Saker, the dauntless pioneer
in the Cameroons; Johann Ludwig Krapf, and Johann
Rebmann, among the greatest Germans to serve with
the C.M.S., intrepid pioneers in Abyssinia and East
Africa, who by their character and example played a
great part in the opening up of the Dark Continent,
and Karl Frederick Gutzlaff, of the Netherlands
Missionary Society, another German, whose adven-
turous journeyings in the China Seas, and voluminous
writings, greatly quickened interest in the Far East;
James Legge, born the year of Waterloo, who, after
important service as an educational missionary in
Hongkong, became Professor of Chinese at Oxford
University, a pioneer in making known to the West the
classics of the East; and, most famous of all, David
Livingstone, " missionary, traveller, philanthropist . . .
for thirty years his life was spent in an unwearied effort

to evangelize the native races, to explore the undiscovered secrets, and to abolish the devastating slave-trade of Central Africa."[1]

Then came those born in the twenty-five years from 1815 to 1841, a period of post-war disillusion, scarcity and depression in England, issuing at last in important political and industrial reforms. Towards the end of this period came the Oxford Movement, the birth of the Anglo-Catholic party in the Church of England, and the abolition of most of the civil disabilities which had attached to Nonconformists, Roman Catholics and Jews since the stormy controversies of the seventeenth century. As might be expected, this generation did not give quite so many leading figures to the mission fields; but to it belonged John G. Paton, the Scottish boy who during his long life in the New Hebrides saw the conversion of no less than twenty thousand natives; Patteson, the noble and gifted martyr-bishop of Melanesia, who was killed in revenge for the kidnapping of natives by traders; and James Chalmers, the restless explorer, also of the South Seas, ever seeking new islands to which to carry the Gospel until finally he was killed and eaten by the wild men of New Guinea. François Coillard and Adolphe Mabille, the great French missionaries of Basutoland, came of the same period, as did James Stewart, of Lovedale, doctor, educational pioneer and missionary statesman, David Hill and Griffith John, daring pioneers in the opening

---

[1] From the inscription on Livingstone's grave in Westminster Abbey. The character and service of Livingstone caught the popular imagination of the Victorian era in a unique manner. To the list of missionary figures born during the Napoleonic war should be added Samuel Crowther, once an African slave, and Thomas Birch Freeman, son of a negro father and an English mother, who both made outstanding contributions to the opening up of the great Niger territories.

up of Central China, and Hudson Taylor, the devoted founder of the China Inland Mission. Nor should Father Damien, the Roman Catholic priest who gave his life for the lepers of Molokai, be forgotten.

The children of the next twenty-five years were ready for the new opportunities brought to the Church by the opening up of Africa and the lands of the Far East. Among them were the dauntless Alexander Mackay, of Uganda, James Hannington, another martyr-bishop—" Tell the King I have purchased the road to Uganda with my life," he said, as he faced the spears of his assailants, " I die for the Baganda "— George Grenfell, the missionary-explorer of the mighty Congo River, and his colleagues, Holman Bentley and Tom Comber. To China, that same early Victorian generation gave James Gilmour, of Mongolia, who set out on what has been described as " the most forlorn hope ever faced by any man, even a missionary,"[1] and Timothy Richard, of whom when he died it was said that " he had left the impress of his own strong personality on an Empire embracing a quarter of the human race."[2] To India went James Anderson Graham, of Kalimpong. Two remarkable women also claim mention in even the most summary list—Mary Slessor, of Calabar, the Scottish mill-girl, who became " the white queen of Okoyong," and Mary Bird, a connection of the Wilberforce family, who went as a pioneer woman worker to Persia and made her way with unusual swiftness and success to the hearts of the proud Moslems.

After these outstanding figures came yet another

[1] *Couriers of Christ*, p. 108.
[2] Cf. Soothill, *Timothy Richard of China*, p. 17; Latourette, *A History of Christian Missions in China*, p. 378.

nineteenth-century generation, some of whom still survive, and all of whose personalities have touched the imagination of our own day—first, the " Cambridge Seven," a group of well-known undergraduates, who under the influence of the evangelist Moody offered themselves to the C.I.M. for service in China;[1] and then, taking the names in order of seniority, Robert Laws, of Livingstonia, and Donald Fraser, one of the pioneers of the Student Volunteer Missionary Union, who built well on the foundation Laws had laid, gaining the native name of *Chisekeseke*, the one " who smiles a smile with everyone "; Theodore Pennell, the doctor who exercised so remarkable an influence on the wild Afghan frontier; Wilfred Grenfell, the famous missionary doctor of Labrador; John R. Mott, who, by ceaseless journeyings in every part of the earth, made outstanding contribution to the expression of modern world-wide Christian fellowship; Frank Weston, the strong missionary Bishop of Zanzibar; C. F. Andrews, friend of Tagore and Gandhi, and the champion of the oppressed everywhere; Temple Gairdner, who poured out his many gifts in the service of the Moslems of Egypt; and Albert Schweitzer, of Lambaréné, musician and philosopher, doctor and theologian.

The mere setting down of the names of this great succession from Carey to Schweitzer indicates something of the amazing variety and vitality of the missionary movement during the nineteenth century. And these are but a few of the more famous figures, whose contribution to the life of their times has given most of them a place, not only in the calendar of the Church, but in standard biographical dictionaries. Behind them stand literally thousands of men and women, who left home

[1] See J. G. Pollock, *The Cambridge Movement*, 1953. chs. v-vi.

and friends to carry the Gospel overseas, and who succeeded, though often at the sacrifice of life itself, in planting the Christian Church in every corner of the earth. " The missionary movement of the past century," says Dr Latourette, " has been the most notable outpouring of life, in the main unselfish, in the service of alien peoples, which the world has ever seen."[1]

Holding the ropes in this country, there stood the great missionary secretaries of the period, men of statesmanlike ability—among them E. B. Underhill and Alfred Henry Baynes of the B.M.S., Wardlaw Thompson of the L.M.S., Henry Venn and Eugene Stock of the C.M.S.—and, co-operating with them, princely givers, of whom one of the best known was Robert Arthington, the strange Leeds recluse, who helped munificently in the evangelization of Africa, and also the poorest of the poor, who gladly and sacrificially supported the cause.

The expansion of the Church in the nineteenth century was not the work of weak sentimentalists, nor of ignorant fanatics, but of the daring, the richly dowered and the strong, men and women made mighty by their faith and by the cause in which they served. They were not of one ecclesiastical pattern or temper, but a company diverse enough to express, in some measure at least, the " multicoloured " wisdom of God.[2]

## IV

Of course there were mistakes and failures. Fallible human beings were setting out into unknown lands on tasks of the greatest difficulty. There was much to

[1] *Missions To-morrow.* Quoted by Kraemer, op. cit., p. 33.
[2] *Ephesians* iii. 10.

learn and a good deal to unlearn. A heavy price in human life had to be paid in almost every field, and sometimes it was made additionally heavy by misguided enthusiasm and carelessness. It was not till 1897 that Sir Ronald Ross after long and complicated researches in India discovered the exact relation between human malaria and mosquitoes. Throughout the whole of the nineteenth century ignorance of how to secure proper protection from this one tropical scourge took grim toll of the missionary band, particularly in Africa. The societies which sought to establish work on the west coast and in the Congo suffered very heavy losses indeed. Missionaries were stricken down one after the other, sometimes after only a few weeks on the field. Moreover, there, and in the South Seas, and in China, indeed almost everywhere, fierce hostility was often encountered from those who misunderstood the purposes of the newcomers, or occasionally from those who understood only too well. The roll of martyrs became at times so lengthy that even missionary enthusiasts queried whether it was right to persist. Carey's generation, however, had recognized that big personal sacrifices might be necessary, and perhaps a number of unsuccessful attempts to enter certain lands. The pioneers were realists, not sentimentalists. David Bogue, when he preached the final sermon at the gatherings which launched the L.M.S., boldly faced the possibility of the failure of the attempt to spread the knowledge of Christ in other parts of the world.[1] Again and again, during the nineteenth century, the missionary movement had to endure scoffing and ridicule from those outside the Church, and not a little drastic criticism

[1] Lovett, i. p. 36.

from those within. Dickens and Thackeray, writing in the eighteen-fifties, represented no insignificant section of their contemporaries, whilst the acute controversy which raged in Methodism in the years 1889-90 had parallels in most other branches of the Church.[1]

These things fall into perspective, however, when one looks at the century as a whole, and sees the splendour of its achievement. Far more resulted from the vision and conviction of the founders of the modern missionary movement than the sending out of Christian pioneers into new lands, and the creation through their efforts of small but scattered Christian communities. The primary aim was the salvation of men and the building up of the world-wide Church of Christ. The measure of what was accomplished may be judged not only from the numerical growth but from the fact that the infant Christian Churches in the South Seas, in Africa and Madagascar, in China and elsewhere, had already at the end of the nineteenth century passed triumphantly through their baptism of blood and fire. It was not only missionaries who had been martyred. Simple believers of every race had shown themselves ready to suffer and die in the name of Christ.

There were, too, many indirect consequences of this striking expansion of the Church. First, there was the effect on the Churches from which the missionaries went out. We have already seen what kind of men the founders of the societies were. They were not neglectful of the dangers through which their country was passing, nor did they forget the needs of their neighbours. They were ready to help with every kind of good work, and

---

[1] Dickens and Thackeray satirized the home supporters—not the missionaries. See Dickens' enthusiastic article on Livingstone in *Household Words*.

to further Christian witness in Britain and on the Continent, as well as in more distant places, believing that only in Christian faith and service, conceived in the widest terms, was there any hope for the future. They gave much thought to evangelism in this country, and the early records of almost all the societies we have been considering give details of special efforts in rural and industrial areas, in Ireland, in France, and in other parts of Europe. And it was soon found that the deepened realization of responsibility for the heathen world overseas, so far from impoverishing the Churches here, gave them a new vitality and earnestness. In sending some of their finest sons overseas they enriched themselves.

Further, the missionary movement was inevitably and rightly involved in many " second-line "[1] activities, and through them made an important contribution not only to its own main purpose but also to the general life of the time. Geographical discovery was obviously greatly assisted by the work of nineteenth-century missionaries. The pioneers had to make their own maps as they pushed their way into uncharted territories, though it was not the mere zest for exploration that carried them there, but obedience to a Voice and compassion for the needy. Particularly was this the case in Africa, where Krapf, Livingstone and Grenfell rendered outstanding service in the opening up of the Dark Continent; but there is hardly any area where missionaries have not an honoured place in the ranks of the cartographers and discoverers.

Even more significant was the missionary contribution to the exploration of the human mind. In almost

---

[1] The phrase is Godfrey Phillips', *The Gospel in the World*, ch. xvi. For the following pages see Latourette, op. cit., vi. pp. 450 f.

all the lands entered missionaries were the pioneers of systematic language study. In many cases, in the South Seas, in Africa and elsewhere, they were the first to reduce primitive languages to writing. Their first concern in this field was the translation of the Bible and adequate provision for Christian worship. The Bible translation work of the nineteenth century forms indeed an epic on its own. By the time it had completed one hundred years' service the Bible Society had published portions of the Scriptures in 76 European languages, 137 Asiatic, 88 African, 28 American and 49 Oceanic— a total of 378. The distribution total for the period was estimated at 186,000,000 copies. To these figures must be added a large amount of Bible translation work undertaken by the separate societies and not, for one reason or another, subsidized by the Bible Society. Behind figures like these there lies concealed long and patient toil, exacting scholarship and often rare human heroism and devotion. Side by side with all this there was the work of the Christian literature and tract societies, which aimed at supplying the more immediate needs of Christian converts and also at providing effective Christian apologetic.

But in many areas the literary achievements of missionaries went far beyond Bible translation and the provision of Christian literature. They were eager to understand more than the language of the peoples they went to, and to penetrate ever deeper into their souls. William Ward, of Serampore, as early as 1811, had ready the first edition, in four substantial volumes, of his comprehensively planned *Account of the Writings, Religion and Manners of the Hindoos, including Translations from their Principal Works*; and from the days of Ward to those of J. N. Farquhar and Nicol Macnicol missionaries have taken the lead in the sympathetic study and exposition of India's religions. James Legge's editions and translations of the Chinese classics remain the basis of modern Chinese studies in the West; he became in 1875 the first professor of Chinese in Oxford University, and almost all his successors have been at one time missionaries. And at the other end of the scale there is the contribution made to the knowledge of primitive peoples. The material out of which the new science of anthropology is slowly taking shape has been largely provided by careful missionary observers.[1] Those who sometimes criticize the Christian Church for the breaches it has made in native custom should recognize how big is the debt owed by primitive peoples and by the learned world to the researches carried on by missionaries.

It is hardly necessary to speak here of the missionary championship of the oppressed and the exploited. When the great societies were founded, the struggle against the slave trade had but recently begun. We have already noted how the personnel of these two great movements overlapped. Wilberforce, Sharp, Macaulay and Hardcastle were outstanding figures in the cause of negro freedom. How big a share they had in the missionary movement we have already seen. Britons were forbidden to engage in the slave trade from 1807, but it was another quarter of a century before emancipation was secured for all the slaves in the British Empire, and in that second phase of the struggle the experiences of John Smith, in Demerara, and of Knibb and his companions in Jamaica, played a great

[1] Cf. F. B. Jevons, *An Introduction to the History of Religion*, p. 6: " The labour which missionaries have bestowed on the study of native religions . . . provides most of the material for the history of early forms of religion."

part in the mobilization of public opinion. In no public question had Carey taken a deeper interest. As a young man he had given up sugar in his tea, " on account of the iniquitous manner in which it is obtained." All his life he referred constantly to the condition of the slaves in his public prayers. In these things he was but typical of those who supported the new societies. Vanderkemp, John Philip and Robert Moffat profoundly influenced the colonial policy of Great Britain towards native races, and David Livingstone called the attention of the whole world to the " open sore " of the Arab slave trade. In the latter part of the nineteenth century, during the scramble of the European Powers for possessions in the newly opened African continent, it was missionaries who again and again took the lead in protesting against shameless iniquities. It was not only racial questions that interested them. The ill-treatment of women and children, the horrors of human sacrifice and cannibalism, of widow-burning and infanticide, the unhappy consequences of caste divisions, the degrading results of indulgence in opium and alcohol —these and many other evils were exposed by the missionaries of the nineteenth century, and active steps taken to bring them to an end.

Education of a literary and scientific character, as we understand it, both in its elementary and higher stages, has been until quite recent times largely the work of missionaries throughout Asia, Africa and the island world. It is estimated that at the end of the nineteenth century the non-Roman societies had in their elementary schools more than a million pupils— over half a million in Asia, 300,000 in Africa, nearly 100,000 in Australasia and the South Seas and some 80,000 in Latin America and the West Indies. In many

cases these figures represented almost all the education
being given in these areas. Further, in the early years
of this century it was claimed that more than one-half
of the total number of arts students in India were in the
colleges connected with the Scottish Churches alone,
and in many parts of Africa the whole educational
system was in Christian hands.[1] That much of the work
was done by rough-and-ready methods, with very
inadequate materials, and that mistakes were made, is
true. Missionary resources were limited. But it must
ever be to the credit of the Church that it recognized
the need, and was brave enough to attempt to meet it.
Particularly important service was rendered in all
areas in the education of women and girls, which till
then had been almost entirely neglected; and in not a
few places valuable industrial training was given.

The missionaries of the nineteenth century were
indeed ready to embark on any line of service which
seemed likely to enlighten and uplift. Carey and his
companions published the first Bengali magazine and
the first vernacular newspaper; they founded the
Agricultural and Horticultural Society of India; they
opened the first savings bank. What they did at
Serampore, other missionaries were doing in other
parts of the world.

Carey and Horne, it will be remembered, appealed
to the Christians of their day to show the same spirit of
enterprise and daring as did traders. If men could
venture across the world in search of wealth or personal
advantage, then surely the Church of Jesus Christ
should send its agents abroad. This challenge was

---

[1] See *Edinburgh Conference Report* (1910), iii., but note that as late as
1889 there was a violent controversy about educational missions in
Methodist circles. See Findlay and Holdsworth, i, ch. vii.

responded to. Missionaries forced their way into India, where, as Dr Findlay puts it, " for two hundred years the natives knew the Englishman as the grasping merchant, the crafty politician, the terrible warrior, before they had the chance of knowing him as the peaceful and beneficent messenger of Christ."[1]

It was the evil reputation of the white man that caused many of the difficulties and dangers met with by the missionary pioneers. As the nineteenth century advanced there came a change. Commerce and colonization began to hold back a little, and then to follow the missionary, taking advantage of the entry he gained into new territories. Sometimes, perhaps, the missionary was rather too willing a tool in this respect. Even the great David Livingstone, speaking in the Senate House in Cambridge in 1857, could define his aims in the famous words: " I go back to Africa to try to make an open path for Commerce and Christianity."[2] Sometimes supporters at home rather too easily identified their religion with their imperialism. It was a religious journal which took leave of one of the great Victorian missionary secretaries with these words: " Among the men who have done most to build up and establish on sure foundations the Empire of which we are rightly proud, there are few, if any, who have played a nobler or more effective part than Mr B——".[3]

[1] Findlay, i. p. 139.

[2] Commerce, however, was thought of by Livingstone as an alternative to the slave trade. Cf. Buxton's motto: " The Bible and the plough must regenerate Africa." Henry Venn, of the C.M.S., did much to foster legitimate trade between England and Nigeria, his aim being the development of Africa's resources in order to end the slave trade.

[3] This was written in 1906. It is perhaps more typical of the first decade of the present century than of any period in the previous hundred years. It may be compared with the opening sentence of one of the chapters in Mrs Creighton's book, *Missions*, 1912, in the Home

But enough has been said in these pages to show how different was the spirit of the missionary pioneers. Even if we have to admit a rather less attractive temper and outlook occasionally as the nineteenth century advanced, it remains true that throughout the whole period the Christian Church in its missionary activity gave to Africa and the East more serious, generous and disinterested service than did any other body of men. Moreover, the verdict of Dr Latourette is significant. " The Christian missions of the nineteenth century," he says, " although often associated closely with commercial and political imperialism, were to a lesser degree tools of that imperialism than in the sixteenth, seventeenth and eighteenth centuries, and even than in the Middle Ages."[1]

The direct expansion of the Church—so rapid and so widespread—and these many indirect consequences! What an amazing sequel to the efforts of those who, during the Napoleonic struggle, recalled Christian people to their missionary obligations! Imagine these things absent from the history of the nineteenth century and how impoverished would be the tale.

v

Dr Latourette describes the nineteenth century as " The Great Century " in the story of the expansion of Christianity. It was, he believes, the century of Christianity's " greatest influence."[2] It may be

University Library: " The critics of missions probably do not realize what a great part they have played and are playing in the spread of civilization." Melvill Horne, *Letters on Missions*, iii., expressly repudiated the " civilizing motive for missions."

[1] *The Unquenchable Light*, 1945, p. 94.

[2] See *A History of the Expansion of Christianity*, iv-v. and iii. p. 457.

regarded as in some respects " pre-eminently the Protestant century,"[1] though there were also important forward moves by the Roman Church in Asia and Africa. Several new missionary orders were established and large sums of money were raised for the propagation of the faith among heathen peoples. While in the sixteenth century leadership in the missionary activity of the Roman Church was largely in the hands of Spaniards and Portuguese, in the nineteenth century it was to a notable extent in the hands of French men and women.

Many of the general characteristics of this great period of Christian advance have already been noted. Some of them deserve re-emphasis and others may be mentioned. There was a comparative absence of Government assistance. " In spite of the intimate connection with the expansion of European, ostensibly Christian peoples," says Latourette, " there was less direction and active assistance from the state than in any era since the beginning of the fourth century."[2] The rank and file of Christian believers became growingly interested in the foreign missionary enterprises of the Churches. A larger part than ever before was played by women. A relatively high standard of belief and conduct was required of converts, and entry into the Church was in most areas an individual rather than a group decision.

Subsequent events have shown that the intensely personal view of conversion and salvation, which was characteristic of the period, had in it elements of weakness as well as strength. In the new lands that were entered by the Christian religion, the converts secured

[1] Ibid, vi. p. 442. Cf. *The Unquenchable Light*, p. 90.
[2] Ibid, vi. p. 443.

were a relatively small percentage of the population. They were isolated from the communities and cultures to which they had belonged, and became dependent not only upon foreign missionaries but upon Western ways of life, remaining too few and too weak to produce a vernacular Christian literature or culture of their own. Nevertheless, their leavening influence was in many lands out of all proportion to their numbers, while the lengthy roll of heroic martyrs proved the strength of the hold which Christianity had secured over certain of its new adherents.

# CHAPTER VII

# INTO THE TWENTIETH CENTURY

" In approaching the world of international disunity
the word of the Church should not be one of advice
but, in a sense, of revelation. It can point to that
unity which God has actually created among men,
and in faith offer it as a token of what might be."
William Paton, *The Church and the New Order*. S.C.M.,
1941, p. 161.

I

THE MISSIONARY SOCIETIES, like the Churches themselves
and most individual Christians, entered the twentieth
century with confidence. They were not fully aware of
what had been accomplished by the Christian faith in
its progress overseas during the previous century, but
all the societies were engaged in new forward enterprises and as one after another celebrated their
centenaries and other special anniversaries, they were
reminded of the spectacular growth of their resources
and commitments, and of new opportunities in every
part of the world. In 1892 an eager young American,
Robert Wilder, had visited Britain and had helped to
inaugurate here the Student Volunteer Missionary
Union, an organization which was already spreading
rapidly in the United States. Its watchword was " The
Evangelization of the World in this Generation." The
bishops of the Anglican Church, when they met at
Lambeth in 1897, wisely resisted the attempt to commit

them to this slogan. So did the leaders of the missionary societies.[1] Nevertheless, the eagerness of the younger generation awakened a widespread response among Christian people, and their programme did not appear entirely fantastic.

Few, if any, then foresaw that the world was entering a new period of revolutionary change; that before many years had passed war in Europe would spread to Asia and Africa and also involve the United States of America; that the conflict would prove but an episode in a still more extended and more desperate struggle; that there would be a widespread repudiation of the Christian faith and of Christian moral standards within those lands which had come to be regarded as part of Christendom, and that rising tides of nationalism in Eastern lands would lead to the revival of ancient religions which had seemed to be dying, if not already dead.

In the early years of the century those directing the missionary enterprises of the Churches in Asia and Africa busied themselves with the working out of closer relationships between the societies, with the development of a common strategy and the establishment of united educational and medical institutions. The World Missionary Conference which met in Edinburgh in 1910 registered and furthered these plans. Carey had proposed " an annual meeting, at the Cape of Good Hope, of all the missionaries in the world." When Henry Martyn, in his first weeks in India in 1806, heard of the project, he noted in his diary that it pleased him very much, " not on account of its practicability, but its grandeur." Andrew Fuller regarded it as the proposal of " an enlarged mind,"

[1] See J. G. Pollock, *The Cambridge Movement*, ch. x.

but did not feel able to approve it. Even in the amended form of a conference every ten years, the first gathering to be held in 1810, it proved no more than a dream. A century later, however, in Edinburgh, the representatives of missionary societies and of Churches overseas met and planned not only for a continuation committee with a permanent staff, but for a series of National Christian Councils representative of all the different groups working in an area.

The National Christian Councils were brought into being through a series of conferences held by Dr John R. Mott on a journey through Asia in 1912-13. Mott had already achieved a considerable reputation as a world evangelist to students. It was he who had presided over the Edinburgh Conference. " The journey of 1912-13 was epoch-making for Christianity," says one of his biographers, " in that it brought into being for the first time not only the framework of world-wide organized relationship between its Churches in their missionary aspect, but created a living fellowship with its roots in the soil, capable of continuous growth."[1] The full significance of Mott's achievement became apparent when it was suddenly and unexpectedly subjected to the strain and stress of the first world war. Many projects had to be abandoned. The supply of missionaries was in many places interrupted. The great German societies were cut off from their mission fields and German missionaries were interned. But the new structure of missionary co-operation survived the conflict, and it proved possible in 1921, within a few years of the end of hostilities, to constitute an International Missionary Council, which rapidly grew in importance and influence. Further journeys by

[1] Basil Mathews, *John R. Mott, World Citizen*, 1934, p. 237.

Mott increased the number of National Christian Councils and strengthened the sense of unity and common purpose in the world mission of the Church. Enlarged meetings of the I.M.C. in Jerusalem in 1928 and at Tambaram, Madras, in 1938 helped so to deepen the sense of fellowship in service that it survived the difficulties and distresses caused by the second world war.

II

In the opening decades of the twentieth century, in spite of the interruptions caused by the two conflicts and in spite of the growing influence of new ideological and social movements hostile to organized Christianity, the younger Churches of Africa and the East grew steadily stronger. There was an impressive numerical growth, and a new indigenous leadership emerged.

The number of missionaries increased. The peak figure for the Protestant Churches was probably reached in 1925. It is estimated that there were then some 22,000 Roman Catholic missionaries serving overseas, and some 28,000 non-Roman missionaries. By 1938, though there were slightly fewer from the non-Roman Churches, the Roman total was considerably higher, and has continued to increase. Dr Latourette notes that " taken the world over, Roman Catholic Christianity has gone forward since 1914 more markedly than has Protestantism,"[1] though the leadership is no longer in French hands as it was in the nineteenth century. But the figures just given for the non-Roman Churches represent a very large increase in the years following the Edinburgh Conference. A much greater share in the missionary enterprise was

[1] *The Unquenchable Light*, p. 109.

taken by the American Churches, and there was also a significant growth in the number of Scandinavian missionaries. In China, for example, in 1895 nearly two-thirds of the missionary force came from Britain, whereas by 1914 about one-half of the number were Americans. In 1895 only between two and three per cent came from the continent of Europe, but by 1914 this figure had increased to ten per cent. Within all these totals the number of women showed a notable rise. It is said that by 1939 considerably over one-third of the foreign missionaries of the Church of England were women, and there were corresponding increases among those of other Churches. Many of the women were, of course, educationists and their number indicates the steady development of schools and colleges overseas. In the early decades of the twentieth century the great Christian universities of China, the Christian colleges of India and notable institutions like Lovedale, Achimota and Mbereshi in Africa grew in influence and importance.

Medical work increased also. A large number of mission hospitals were opened, and much valuable research was carried on under missionary auspices. The Mission to Lepers (1874), and other societies doing medical work, gave special attention, with marked success—particularly of recent years—to leprosy, the most pitiable of endemic diseases. Rural dispensaries have been established, hygiene and health campaigns initiated. Fifty years ago separately organized medical work was a new feature subject to some criticism among the supporters of the larger missionary societies. It has now a major place in most programmes. So many women are serving abroad as doctors and nursing sisters that it comes as something of a shock to discover that the first nursing sister sent out by the C.M.S. was commissioned as recently as 1890 and the first woman doctor in 1895. Names such as Dugald Christie and Thomas Cochrane, Sir Albert Cook and Sir Henry Holland, Harold Balme, Howard Somervell and Clement Chesterman, Dame Edith Brown and Dr Ida Scudder tell of the highest professional skill allied to deep missionary consecration.

The growth of missionary personnel and the development of education and medical services are, however, less important than the increase in the number of converts. In the first three decades of the century the membership of the Churches connected with non-Roman missions multiplied four-fold. In India there were a number of " mass movements " into the Christian Church. There were striking gains in almost every part of Africa south of the Sahara. Strong Christian communities emerged in the Philippines, in Burma, in Sumatra and in many of the islands of the Pacific. The Churches in China grew steadily in strength and influence up to the time of the seizure of power by the Communists, in spite of the disturbance of life caused by revolution, civil war and the Sino-Japanese conflict. Ordained members of the younger Churches more than trebled between 1911 and 1938, and leaders appeared who were known and acclaimed far beyond their own lands. A Bishop Crowther and a King Khama were isolated figures in the nineteenth century, but in the past fifty years a noble succession has taken its place in the calendar of the world-wide Church—Aggrey of Africa, Sadhu Sundar Singh, Bishop Azariah of Dornakal, Ch'eng Ching-Yi of China, Kagawa of Japan, D. T. Niles of Ceylon, and many others. They are striking evidence of " the

deeper rooting of the Faith on its geographic frontiers."[1]
It is perhaps more than a coincidence that just as
Tertullian and Cyprian began the tradition of outstanding Latin leadership in the Church a century and
a half after Christianity set out on its mission in the
Mediterranean world, so men like these appeared a
century and a half after the birth of the modern
missionary movement.

At the Edinburgh Conference of 1910, those of
Asiatic and African birth were a mere handful among
the 1,200 delegates, and they were regarded almost as
curiosities. At the Jerusalem meeting of the International Missionary Council eighteen years later, one
in every four of those present was of other than white
race. At Madras, in 1938, more than half the conference
represented the native leadership of the younger
Churches; and the delegates from India, China, Japan
and many parts of Africa and elsewhere spoke with
conspicuous authority and power. In the ecumenical
conferences held since the second world war—at
Amsterdam, Lund and Evanston—an increasingly
important contribution has been made by those
from the younger Churches. Slowly but surely the
Churches overseas have been taking their place in the
Church Universal.

### III

This process has been aided by other developments
to which the Edinburgh Conference gave an important
impetus. The twentieth century has seen a steady
growth in Christian co-operation and unity in many
other fields besides that of missionary endeavour.

Bishop Brent of the American Episcopal Church

[1] Latourette, *Interpretative Statistical Survey*, p. 239.

went home from Edinburgh convinced that increased missionary co-operation would speedily necessitate a franker facing of the problems connected with Faith and Order on which the various Christian traditions were divided. For the sake of the Churches of Africa and the East, as well as for their own sake, the Churches of the West ought, so it seemed to him, to meet together to discuss theological and ecclesiological issues. Much patient preparation was necessary before he achieved his object and his plans were delayed by the first world war. At length, however, in 1927 in Lausanne the first World Conference on Faith and Order was held.[1] Thirteen of the Orthodox Eastern Churches were represented, thirteen Churches of the Anglican communion, five groups of Baptists, five groups of Congregationalists, fourteen Lutheran Churches, twenty-two Churches of the Presbyterian and Reformed tradition, the seven Evangelical Churches of Germany, twelve Methodist groups, together with representatives of the Brethren of America, the Disciples of Christ, the Friends, the Moravians, the Mennonites, the Old Catholics, the Czechoslovak Church and two or three others. Among the delegates were a number of nationals from India, China and Japan.

The discussions begun at Lausanne were continued at another conference in Edinburgh in 1937 and a third World Conference on Faith and Order was held at Lund in Sweden in 1952.[2] The problems which have had to be faced in these conferences are thorny and difficult ones. They include the doctrine of grace

[1] See E. S. Woods, *Lausanne 1927*.
[2] See E. H. Robertson, *Lund 1952*, and O. S. Tomkins, *The Third World Conference on Faith and Order*, 1953.

and varied conceptions of the ministry and sacraments. Increasingly, attention has had to be focused on the doctrine of the Church itself, and as the years have passed Christian leaders from Asia and Africa have taken a more and more prominent part in the discussions. At Edinburgh in 1910 Churches and missionary societies entered into " comity " agreements to respect one another's fields of operation. But as the Churches overseas have grown and Christians from one area have moved into another, the necessity of new and closer Church relations has become apparent. The younger Churches have not unnaturally shown themselves impatient of the divisions to which Europe and America have long become accustomed and which, though they represent diverse theological interpretations and emphases, seem less significant in missionary lands.

Moreover, the twentieth century has seen the formation of a number of United Churches. Sometimes these have resulted from the coming together of groups belonging to the same ecclesiastical family. In other cases, however, Churches of different traditions have decided to unite. The United Church of Canada, which came into existence in 1924, was a union of Presbyterians, Congregationalists and Methodists. The South India United Church, which was represented at the Lausanne Conference, had been constituted in 1908 of Christian congregations connected with five separate missions, those of the London Missionary Society, the American Board of Commissioners for Foreign Missions, the Church of Scotland, the United Free Church of Scotland and the Dutch Reformed Church in America. After many years of negotiations this South India United Church joined in 1947 with the Methodist Church

and with certan dioceses of the (Anglican) Church
of India, Burma and Ceylon to inaugurate the Church
of South India, a much more inclusive and significant
union of episcopal and formerly non-episcopal Churches.[1]
In Ceylon, in North India, and in certain parts of
Africa, as well as in Britain and the United States,
Churches have entered into serious discussions regarding
new and closer relationships.[2] The way forward has
proved difficult, for the Churches are divided not only
by sincerely held convictions but by ways of worship,
and by the social and cultural factors, which have
helped to create for each of them a familiar and loved
*ethos*, not lightly changed or surrendered.

From Edinburgh 1910 there came yet another stream
of Christian collaboration and consultation, that known
as the Life and Work Movement. In Stockholm in
1925, on the initiative and under the leadership of
Archbishop Söderblom, of Uppsala, there was held
the Universal Christian Conference on Life and Work.
It was concerned primarily with the relationship of
the Church to the social order and with economic,
social and international problems. The Continuation
Committee appointed at Stockholm decided to convene
in Oxford in 1937 a World Conference on Church,
Community and State.[3] Delegates were sent by all the
principal Churches in the United States, in Great
Britain, in the British Dominions, and on the continent
of Europe. The Eastern Orthodox Churches and the
Old Catholics were represented. There were also
delegates from the younger Churches in Japan, China,
India, Africa and South America.

[1] See Marcus Ward, *The Pilgrim Church*, 1953
[2] See Stephen Neill, *Towards Church Union 1937-1952*.
[3] See *The Churches Survey their Task*, 1937.

The three streams of missionary co-operation, of theological discussion and of joint social witness flowed for a time side by side. But the need to co-ordinate them soon became apparent. Christian leaders found themselves inevitably involved in all these movements and the spheres overlapped, even though certain Churches did not find it possible to support all three movements with equal enthusiasm. It was agreed in 1937 that " with a view to facilitating the more effective action of the Christian Church in the modern world, the movements known as ' Life and Work ' and ' Faith and Order ' should be more closely related in a body representative of the Churches and caring for the interests of each movement." From this decision came the plans for a World Council of Churches. The successful drafting of the constitution owed much to the wisdom and authority of Dr William Temple, then Archbishop of York. The second world war delayed the inauguration of the World Council, but in 1948 at an Assembly in Amsterdam it was formally constituted. One hundred and fifty-eight churches of forty-four different lands became foundation members, declaring that they had come together and intended to stay together for mutual strengthening and service, and in order to discover the way towards fuller Christian unity. The International Missionary Council associated itself with the World Council, and the two bodies quickly found themselves involved in ever closer relationships.

Six years after its formation, the World Council of Churches held its second Assembly. This met at Evanston, near Chicago, in 1954. There were 1,298 participants from 179 Churches in 54 countries. The Assembly provided striking evidence of how quickly

the World Council has established itself as an in-
strument for Christian fellowship and joint witness.
" It is not a Super-Church. It is not the World Church.
It is not the *Una Sancta* of which the Creeds speak."[1]
But it is, as the General Secretary, Dr Visser't Hooft,
has said, " a body in and through which, when it
pleases God, a foretaste of the *Una Sancta* is given."
During the first six years of its life, the Council found
itself in a period of swift and sometimes dramatic
change in world affairs. It successfully undertook a
large programme of inter-Church aid and service for
refugees in Central Europe, in the Middle East and
the Far East, and in numerous ways drew the member
Churches together for united thought and action.

From the standpoint of the younger Churches—and
the older Churches as well—not the least significant of
its early decisions was the appointment in 1951,
jointly with the International Missionary Council, of
Dr Rajah B. Manikam as East Asia Secretary. So
valuable did this appointment prove that the Evanston
Assembly decided to make similar appointments in
other areas as part of the plans for the closer integra-
tion of the International Missionary Council and the
various National Christian Councils with the work of the
World Council.

IV

Delegates from the Lutheran and Evangelical
Churches of Germany were unable to secure permission
from the Nazi authorities to attend the Oxford
Conference on Church, Community and State. The

---

[1] " The Church, the Churches and the World Council of Churches."
Statement adopted by the Central Committee at Toronto, July 1950.
See also G. K. A. Bell, *The Kingship of Christ*, Penguin Books, 1954.

outbreak of war between China and Japan over-
shadowed the Madras meeting of the International
Missionary Council in 1938. In Russia both Orthodox
and Evangelical believers had been for several years
subject to hostile pressure from the Soviet authorities.
It was already apparent, even before the outbreak of
the second world war, that new forces were at work in
the world inimical to the life and witness of the Church.

These forces increased in range and strength as a
result of the conflict of 1939-45. Both Roman and non-
Roman Churches in Europe were subject to persecution
first by the Nazi régime and then by that of the Soviets.
Foreign missionaries had to leave many parts of China
in the face of the Japanese advance, and though they
quickly returned after 1945, within a few years they
were ousted again by the Chinese Communist authorities. German missions were once more " orphaned "
and German missionary activity brought to a stop.
Nevertheless, the Churches of Asia, Africa and the
South Seas showed a remarkable sturdiness and
resilience in the face of the troubles and upheavals to
which they were subjected, and the structure of
international and inter-confessional Christian relationships built up in the early decades of the century
proved strong enough to stand the strain imposed
upon it.

In 1942 a British aeroplane crashed near the
Chindwin River in Burma. The only survivor was a
nineteen-year-old R.A.F. sergeant gunner. He was
found and cared for by a friendly Burmese who took
him one day to a village church which he said had not
been visited by a white man for seven years. Gathering
a congregation, he asked the airman to preach to them.
When, a week or so later, the young man was able to

rejoin his unit, he related his experiences and said that the congregation included four Chinese soldiers. " I made a kind of speech to them," he said, " telling the villagers what Britain was like, and of my travels in the R.A.F."[1] The story could be paralleled by many incidents which occurred during the campaigns in the Pacific and elsewhere. As a result of the heroic labours of missionaries, the Christian Church is now represented in almost every land. Though weak in many places, it is growingly conscious of its unity and determined to express it better. But it has to face not only active persecution and the challenge of its claims by older faiths allied to new nationalisms, but also the loosening of its hold on many in the lands where formerly it was strong. Within Christendom many are no longer convinced Christians or concerned about the Christian mission.

There have been, that is to say, losses as well as gains. So competent an observer as Dr Latourette is certain that the gains, even though they be mainly on the frontiers of the faith, outweigh the losses. Never has any faith been so rooted among so many peoples as is Christianity today. It has been proved that the appeal of Jesus Christ is universal, and of that we could not have been so sure from observed experience a century and a half ago. The day of missionary societies of the nineteenth-century type may be drawing to a close, but the task they set themselves is unfinished and the mission of the Church remains what it has always been, to make disciples of all nations. In this task the East can now aid the West, as well as the West the East. The first half of the twentieth century has made this clear, and has also driven the Church to a re-examination

[1] *Times*, June 19th, 1942.

of its own essential nature and resources, as well as its methods. Mr David Paton is not alone in the view that "the ending of the missionary era in China by Communist *force majeure* is to be understood as the execution of the will of God, albeit through those who not only do not recognize Him but deny His existence."[1] But this does not mean that the mandate of the Church is withdrawn. What seems to some to be the end provides the opportunity for a new beginning, which requires men and women as daring and devoted as those who were the human instruments in bringing into existence the world-wide Christian fellowship of our day.

[1] *Christian Missions and the Judgment of God*, p. 18.

# CHAPTER VIII

# THE CALLING OF THE CHURCH

" Evangelism, missionary work, the proclamation of
the Gospel to earth's remotest end, are not extras or
fringes on the ecumenical movement; they are
essentials without which its true value cannot be
grasped." Stephen Neill, *A History of the Ecumenical
Movement.* S.P.C.K., 1954, p. 730.

I

DURING THE BOMBING of London in September 1940,
the Natural History Museum at South Kensington was
hit. Some of the exhibits were lost altogether. Some
that were rescued from fire were damaged by water.
Among the latter was a small box of seeds of a plant
allied to mimosa. The interest of this particular exhibit
lay in the fact that the seeds were collected in China in
1793 by Sir George Staunton. When, two months
after the air raid, the box was opened, it was found that
a number of them had begun to germinate. Three of
the seedlings were at once sent to the Chelsea Physic
Garden, but within a few weeks two of them were lost
as a result of another enemy attack on London. The
third seedling grew into a sturdy plant. After being
dry for 147 years it still had life within it.

The year 1793 was the year William Carey arrived
in India to begin a notable new chapter in the history
of the Christian Church. Though more than a century
has passed since his death, his is a name that still has
spiritual life and challenge within it, and the same is

true of the names of his missionary-minded contemporaries, who in a time of war and revolutionary change gave themselves to the carrying of the Gospel to lands where the Christian faith was then unknown.

Church history has often been recorded in terms of theologians and ecclesiastics. Attention has been concentrated on disputes and controversies, on the schisms and heresies, on religious wars and the like. The missionaries of the Church and the slow but steady expansion of the faith have received scant attention. Yet from the time of the apostles to our own day, the life of the Church has depended on the faithful witnessing in season and out of season of those who have believed with Carey that the commission given by the Lord Jesus Christ to his disciples continues binding on all Christians.[1] Those who have eagerly and joyfully sought to fulfil the commission, often at great cost to themselves, have extended the frontiers of the faith in all directions.

The New Testament shows how swiftly and effectively in the first century the good news was carried westwards through the Mediterranean world from Jerusalem to Rome. It provides, unfortunately, only a few hints of the parallel movement eastwards to Babylon and beyond and southwards into Egypt; yet the early literature of the Church makes it clear that within a few decades of the Crucifixion the message was known in places very remote from the Mediterranean. Of the successors of the apostles, Eusebius, the first Church historian, writing early in the fourth century, tells us:

" Very many . . . whose heart had been ravished by the divine Word with a burning love for

[1] See *The Enquiry*, 1792.

'philosophy' [i.e. Christian asceticism], had first fulfilled the command of the Saviour and divided their
goods among the needy. Then they set out on long
journeys, performing the office of evangelists,
eagerly striving to preach Christ to those who as yet
had never heard the word of faith, and to deliver to
them the holy gospels. In foreign lands they simply
laid the foundations of the faith. That done, they
appointed others as shepherds, entrusting them
with the care of the new growth, while they themselves proceeded with the divine grace and co-
operation to other countries and to other peoples."[1]

Not a few of these early missionaries must have laid
down their lives, as did so many in the Roman Empire
when the systematic persecution of Christians began.
But, as Harnack put it, " every confessor and martyr
was a missionary; he not merely confirmed the faith of
those who were already won, but also enlisted new
members by his testimony and his death. . . . Nevertheless, it was not merely the confessors and martyrs
who were missionaries. It was characteristic of this
religion that everyone who seriously confessed the faith
proved of service to its propaganda."[2]

Such glowing zeal was not everywhere maintained
for very long. There came periods when the Church
lost its vision and enthusiasm. Again and again,
however, through the centuries new missionary im-
pulses arose and there has never been a time when
some Christians have not had within their hearts the
desire to win fresh territories and people for the faith.
Even those judged unorthodox, because of the influence

---

[1] Eusebius, *Ecclesiastical History*, iii. 37. 2.

[2] *The Expansion of Christianity in the First Three Centuries*, E.T.1904, i.
pp. 458-60.

among them of the teachings of an Arius and a Nestorius, made a notable contribution to the spread of the Christian religion. Many centuries later, some of the medieval " heretics," and Reformation groups like the Anabaptists, showed a missionary concern and zeal far greater than that of their Christian persecutors. In every age there have been those who have taken the Great Commission seriously and have claimed the fulfilment of the promise which attaches to it. In spite of unfavourable circumstances, in spite of national and racial prejudices, which are always difficult to over-come, in spite of theological misconceptions, in spite of many dangers, individual Christians have shown that they believe with one of the early Puritans that " we are to labour by all possible means to bring home the Jews and the Turks, and all other barbarous nations where we traffic, to the knowledge and love of the truth: that they may partake in this righteousness which Christ hath wrought for as many of them as appertain to his election."[1]

## II

The previous pages have set forth in some detail the story of the modern missionary movement, and in particular the striking growth of the Church since the end of the eighteenth century. There are now, accord-ing to Dr Latourette, organized Christian communities in every land save Outer Mongolia, Afghanistan and Nepal, and it may well be that even there individual believers are to be found.

The missionary task is not, however, completed. Carey argued that the command of Christ must remain

[1] John Smyth, *The Bright Morning Star*, 1603 (*The Works of John Smyth*, edited by W. T. Whitley, 1915, i. p. 65).

binding unless it be repealed, unless it be impossible
of fulfilment, and unless there be " no subjects in the
world for the commanded act to be exercised upon."[1]
None of those conditions is yet fulfilled  When Carey
wrote his *Enquiry*, the Christian religion was practically
confined to Europe and the eastern seaboard of
the American continent  There were left few vital
centres of the Roman Catholic missions of the sixteenth
century, and of the ancient Church of South India,
which traces its history back to the work of the Apostle
Thomas, Carey knew nothing. In little more than a
century and a half the situation has been transformed.
But in the East and the West the need for missionary
endeavour remains.

In many parts of the world the Christians are few in
number. Their knowledge of the faith is rudimentary.
Local leadership is weak. The pull back to paganism is
strong. Ancient faiths such as Hinduism and Buddhism
have again become actively propagandist, often making
use of missionary methods similar to those employed by
Christians. The forces of secularism wean men and
women from any kind of religious observance or understanding. In some lands there have been of recent years
deliberate and militant anti-religious movements.
Even in places where there has long been Christian
witness and the number of professing Christians is
considerable, there have been signs of debility and
apostasy. So long as this is the situation Christians of
every race and tradition must continue to heed the
command to make disciples, teaching them to observe
all the words of Christ.

The situation is constantly changing, but in its
essentials it remains the same. The foreign missionary

[1] *The Enquiry*, 1792, pp. 9 and 10.

force may have to be re-deployed, but it is still needed. From certain lands it may, temporarily at any rate, be banished. In others its work may be restricted to certain special types of activity. But even so Christian witness-bearing must go on. Christian doctors, teachers, writers, agriculturalists and technicians are still greatly needed and eagerly welcomed in many parts of the world. Even if the Church has, in some places, to bring to an end the kind of work undertaken by the missionary societies founded in the nineteenth century, it may find new means of bearing witness to its faith and perhaps new spheres of service. All too often the work of foreign missionaries has been hampered, if not made entirely ineffective, by the behaviour of those who have gone overseas as travellers and as business men. Even greater has been the hindrance caused by the unchristian conduct of those in Europe and America towards Asiatics and Africans seeking education or employment overseas. The call for missionary recruits is still insistent. The type of service that may be rendered is perhaps more varied than ever before. Often it is within the home community that evangelistic and missionary effort is needed. " The most numerous and successful missionaries of the Christian religion," said Harnack of the early centuries, " were not the regular teachers but Christians themselves, by dint of their loyalty and courage."[1]

### III

It is disturbing to have the foreign missionary force driven from China and Persia, even if it be only temporarily; to see barriers erected against new

[1] *The Expansion of Christianity*, i. p. 458.

recruits and new societies entering India and other lands; to be cut off from fellow-Christians by political considerations and to hear stories of persecution and imprisonment; to see Christians separated by racial and ethnic tensions. This is not, however, the first time that such things have occurred and God has His own ways of making the wrath of man praise Him.

Most foreign missionaries had to leave North China on the outbreak in 1937 of the Sino-Japanese war. After a few years' absence they were able to return. The Chinese Christians had passed through a period of great difficulty and tribulation, but they had not been silenced or scattered. In many places the Churches were, in the opinion of the missionaries, stronger and more vigorous because they had been deprived of outside aid and had been driven back upon their own resources and those indicated to them in the Bible. A new kind of organization emerged, closer in many respects to the pattern set forth in the New Testament. Loyalty and courage, supported by the assurance that friends overseas were praying for them, had enabled Chinese Christians to maintain their witness, and they even had stories to tell of contact with Japanese soldiers who shared their faith in Christ. Similar things have often happened in Christian history and will happen again.

In this connection the story of Christian witness in Soviet Russia is significant. Under the Czars Christianity was represented almost solely by the ancient Orthodox Church and this Church was closely linked with the Government. Those who professed other forms of Christianity were subject to attack and persecution. But German settlers of evangelical persuasion who went to the Ukraine carried their faith

with them and not only maintained their own ways of
worship but converted a number of Russians, who
became fearless evangelists among their own people.
Many of these Russians suffered imprisonment and
exile to Siberia. No official recognition was given to
dissenting groups until the revolution of 1905 and it
was not until that of 1917 that they had anything
approaching religious freedom. But they bravely
persisted in their witness and by 1917 there were at
least 100,000 baptised believers in Russia. During the
first ten years of the Communist régime they had
opportunities they had never known before. The
Orthodox Church was in disfavour because of its close
association with the Czarist Government. Baptists and
Evangelicals had suffered, as had the political rebels,
and so were viewed with more sympathy. But from
1927 onwards the Soviet authorities attacked all
religious bodies, whether Christian, Jewish or Moslem.
A militant anti-God campaign was sponsored. Anti-
God museums were opened. The Communist leaders
proclaimed themselves atheists and sought to stamp
out religion, which they said was, as Karl Marx had
suggested, the opium of the people.

For nearly fifteen years Russian Christians suffered
grievously and their ranks were sadly thinned. Those
who protested were sent to labour camps. It seemed
that organized religion was to disappear and that a new
generation would grow up successfully indoctrinated
with atheism and irreligion. Then came the second
world war. Large parts of the Soviet Union were
overrun by the Germans. Casualties were extremely
heavy and there was great material damage. Men and
women were soon in desperate need of spiritual consola-
tion. The leaders of the anti-God movement had had

apparent success, but in reality they had failed, like earlier persecutors of the faith. Slowly but surely the remnants of the Orthodox Church and of the evangelical movement were able to show themselves again. First in one place, then in another, churches were reopened and soon had large congregations.

The last ten years have been years of renewed progress. The climate of opinion has been changing again and so has official policy. Religious work has to be carried on within strictly defined limits, but the Churches are again in the open. There is freedom of worship and Christians can appeal to the authorities if their services are interrupted. There can be no organized religious instruction of the young and any kind of political disaffection is vigorously suppressed. There is not what the West would call full religious freedom. To the outside world and to the casual visitor it may appear that the new Russia has no place for religion, but he who seeks finds. The Orthodox Church has been sadly stricken, but there are now within it many signs of new life. The Baptists and Evangelical Christians are united in a union which comprises over 5,000 churches with over 512,000 members. These churches are to be found in all parts of the Soviet Union from Leningrad to the Caucasus, from Moscow to Eastern Siberia. They are made up not only of old people but of the young and the middle-aged. With few Bibles and hymn books, and none of the aids to Christian propaganda so plentiful in Britain and the United States, the faith has been maintained and spread by the personal testimony of individuals.

What has been happening in the Soviet Union can happen in Communist China and in other lands.

There is of course no guarantee that particular Churches or organized groups will survive. The Christianity of North Africa succumbed completely before the Moslem invaders of the seventh and eighth centuries. Christian Churches have been planted in China on at least two previous occasions and almost all trace of them has vanished. Survival depends on the real rooting of the faith in the hearts and lives of individuals and on the missionary zeal of the individual believer. But the same is true of the Christianity of Western Europe and of America. Every Christian Church is embedded in and to some extent conditioned and shaped by the community around it. National peculiarities and political considerations have their influence not only on the setting but on the character of its witness. Many of the tensions and divisions between the Churches, which appear to stem from differences of doctrine and polity, are perpetuated, if not caused, by what Professor C. H. Dodd in a letter he wrote in 1949 described as " non-theological factors." Social, cultural and ideological influences are at work, now as always, in the life of the Church as well as in society and in international relationships.

These things emphasize " the calling of the Church to Mission and Unity," that is, to its obligation to take the Gospel to the whole world and to draw all Christ's people together. The Central Committee of the World Council of Churches drew attention to this double obligation at a meeting in 1951 and declared that:

" every attempt to separate these two tasks violates the wholeness of Christ's ministry to the world. Both of them are, in the strict sense of the word, essential to the being of the Church and the fulfilment of its function as the Body of Christ."[1]

In 1952 an enlarged meeting of the International Missionary Council, held at Willingen in Germany, issued a parallel declaration:

" The calling of the Church to mission and unity issues from the nature of God Himself, made known to us in the whole biblical revelation of the work and purpose of God in Christ. God has made of one blood all nations of men. In Christ we see God's redemptive action; in Christ God is still at work reconciling all things to Himself in one restored humanity. Christ called His apostles that they might be one with Him and with one another, and that He might send them forth, to share with Him His mission for the redemption of the world. The calling of the Church is to be one family in Him and to make known to the whole world, in word and deed, His gospel of the Kingdom. Christ prayed for His disciples that they might be one in Him, as He and the Father are one, that the world might believe that the Father had sent Him."

The Christians of the world must not allow themselves to be separated from one another. They must constantly strive for closer understanding and fellowship, bridging the gulfs created by differences of race and nationality, social organization and political outlook, theological emphasis, church polity and ways of worship. They have to learn to speak the truth to one another in love that they may " grow up in every way into Him who is the head into Christ."[2] And at the

[1] See *The First Six Years 1948-54. Report of the Central Committee of the World Council of Churches*, p. 127.

[2] *Ephesians* iv. 15, R.S.V.

same time they must remember their obligation to carry the whole Gospel to the whole world. This involves witness-bearing within their own communities, to their own people, and also to those of all other races and nations.

In his *Enquiry*, from which a number of quotations have been made in these pages, William Carey described the character of a Christian minister as he understood it. In the New Testament the words "minister" and "ministry" are not used in any professional sense. They are applied to the character and service of all Christians. Carey's words have therefore a wider reference than he gave them in his famous pamphlet.

"A Christian minister is a person who in a peculiar sense is *not his own*; he is the *servant* of God, and therefore ought to be wholly devoted to him. . . . He solemnly undertakes to be always engaged, as much as possible, in the Lord's work, and not to choose his own pleasure, or employment, or pursue the ministry as a something that is to subserve his own ends, or interests, or as a kind of bye-work. . . . The slights and hatred of men, and even pretended friends, gloomy prisons and tortures, the society of barbarians of uncouth speech, miserable accommodations in wretched wildernesses, hunger and thirst, nakedness, weariness, and painfulness, hard work, and but little worldly encouragement, should rather be the objects of their expectation. Thus the apostles acted, in the primitive times, and endured hardness, as good soldiers of Jesus Christ; and though we living in a civilized country where Christianity is protected by law, are not called to suffer these things while we continue here, yet I question whether all are justified in staying here, while so many are perishing without means of grace in other lands."[1]

Carey wrote those words some time before he set out for India. He and his fellow-missionaries of all ages and climes have provided many an illustration of their truth. They are still true. All are not justified in staying in their native lands, for there is still much to be done in carrying the Gospel overseas and in ministering to the stability, growth and unity of the Church throughout the world. In a letter written to one of his sons in 1821, Carey used other words that are applicable to all Christians whether they find their sphere of service in their own or some other land: " May you and I, my dear Jabez, always keep in view our character, our obligations and our vast responsibility, and let us spend and be spent for God."

[1] *Enquiry*, pp. 72-3.

# SELECTED BIBLIOGRAPHY

## (1) General

K. S. LATOURETTE. *A History of the Expansion of Christianity*, vols. i-vii. London, 1938-45.

K. S. LATOURETTE. *The Unquenchable Light*. London, 1945.

R. LOVETT. *A Primer of Modern Missions*. London, 1896.

M. L. G. CARUS-WILSON. *The Expansion of Christendom*. London, 1910.

L. CREIGHTON. *Missions*. London, 1912.

C. H. ROBINSON. *History of Christian Missions*. Edinburgh, 1915.

RUTH ROUSE. *God Has a Purpose*. London, 1935.

JOHN FOSTER. *World Church*. London, 1945.

E. E. WHITE. *The Story of Missions*. New York, 1925.

*Interpretative Statistical Survey of the World Mission of the Christian Church*. London and New York, 1938.

M. SEARLE BATES. *Data on the Distribution of the Missionary Enterprise*. International Missionary Council. 1943.

H. MARTIN and E. A. PAYNE. *A Christian Year Book*. London, 1950.

HENDRIK KRAEMER. *The Christian Message in a Non-Christian World*. London, 1938.

GODFREY PHILLIPS. *The Gospel in the World*. London, 1939

MAX WARREN. *The Christian Mission*. London, 1951.

DAVID M. PATON. *Christian Missions and the Judgment of God*. London, 1953.

## (2) The History of the Societies

C. F. PASCOE. *Two Hundred Years of the S.P.G.* London, 1901.

H. P. THOMPSON. *Into All Lands: The History of the S.P.G. 1701-1950*. London, 1951.

W. F. FRANCE. *The Oversea Episcopate.* London, 1941.

*The Advance Guard: Two Hundred Years of Moravian Missions.* London, 1932.

F. A. COX. *History of the Baptist Missionary Society from 1792 to 1842.* 2 vols. London, 1842.

*The Centenary Volume of the Baptist Missionary Society.* London, 1892.

F. TOWNLEY LORD. *Achievement: A Popular History of the B.M.S.* London, 1942.

R. LOVETT. *History of the London Missionary Society, 1795-1895.* 2 vols. London, 1899.

NORMAN GOODALL. *A History of the L.M.S., 1895-1945.* O.U.P., 1954.

C. SILVESTER HORNE. *The Story of the L.M.S.* London, 1908.

E. A. PAYNE. *Before the Start: Steps towards the founding of the L.M.S.* London, 1942.

J. C. HARRIS. *Couriers of Christ.* London, 1931.

EUGENE STOCK. *The History of the Church Missionary Society.* 3 vols. London, 1899.

R. E. DOGGETT. *C.M.S. through the Years.* London, 1941.

J. MACLEOD CAMPBELL. *Christian History in the Making.* London, 1946.

W. CANTON. *A History of the British and Foreign Bible Society.* 5 vols. London, 1904-10.

G. G. FINDLAY and W. W. HOLDSWORTH. *The History of the Wesleyan Methodist Missionary Society.* 5 vols. London, 1921.

G. G. and M. FINDLAY. *Wesley's World Parish.* London, 1913.

F. PRATT GREEN. *Methodism and the Mountain Summit.* London, 1932.

R. W. WEIR. *Foreign Missions of the Church of Scotland.* Edinburgh, 1900.

D. MACKICHAN. *The Missionary Ideal in the Scottish Churches.* London, 1927.

MARSHALL BROOMHALL. *The Jubilee Story of the C.I.M., 1865-1915.* London, 1915.

G. H. WILSON. *The History of the Universities' Mission to Central Africa.* London, 1936.

SERGE BOLSHAKOFF. *The Foreign Missions of the Russian Orthodox Church.* London, 1943.

ROLAND OLIVER. *The Missionary Factor in East Africa.* London, 1953.

T. S. JOHNSON. *The Story of a Mission. The Sierra Leone Church.* London, 1953.

# INDEX